RADICAL
CLARITY

AMANDA,
MAKE ROOM FOR
MEANING!

RADICAL CLARITY

How Accidental CEOs
Uncover Meaning,
Lead with Purpose,
and Accelerate Growth

PETE STEEGE

Copyright © 2025 by Pete Steege

Published by Kalla House Press

All rights reserved. No part of this publication may be reproduced, distributed or transmitted in any form or by any means, including photocopying, recording, or other electronic or mechanical methods, without the prior written permission of the author, except in the case of brief quotations embodied in critical reviews and certain other noncommercial uses permitted by copyright law. For permission requests, write to the author, addressed "Attention: Permissions Coordinator," at the email address below.

Pete Steege
pete@b2b-clarity.com
www.b2b-clarity.com

Radical Clarity, Pete Steege —1st ed.
ISBN: 979-8-9868533-5-2 (hardback)
ISBN: 979-8-9868533-4-5 (paperback)

PRAISE FOR RADICAL CLARITY

Pete Steege has written the rare C-suite business book that is as insightful as it is actionable. Pete is the real deal when it comes to turning C-level vision into tactical action and lasting results. If you need strategic clarity and serious business momentum, he's the partner you want in your corner. No one does it better.

-David Newman, Author,
Do It! Marketing and Do It! Selling

Radical Clarity is a must-read for high-growth company leaders who find themselves at the helm, navigating growth, challenges, and opportunities—often without a roadmap. Pete helps business leaders turn unexpected responsibility into remarkable success.

-Ian Charpentier, Founder, AccelerateHR Solutions

We are so grateful for Pete. He put us on the path to identify markets and approaches we would not have found on our own and organized the way we think about our business. The practice of Radical Clarity couldn't have come at a more opportune time for us and has changed everything.

-Elliot Tan, CEO, Think Tank

Pete has a unique ability to cut through complexity and uncover the deeper meaning that drives both personal and organizational growth. His insights have consistently led to transformative breakthroughs that go far beyond marketing, shaping lasting success for CEOs and their businesses.

–Chris Heim, CEO, Atomic Data

Pete is the rare business guide and growth strategist that helps technology-driven engineering-focused firms achieve product, company, culture, and brand alignment with their market, ramp up growth, and unlock value.

–Tim Butler, Founder, GrowthFire

Every time I work with Pete, I learn something new. His ability to communicate complex ideas simply makes him a standout leader and partner.

–Sherman Black, CEO, TruGrit360

Our business was experiencing growth, but at times, it felt like we were trying to do too much. Pete helped us identify and define what truly set us apart from our competitors and narrowed our focus to further enhancing our existing strengths. Working with Pete has been beneficial to our business and to me personally.

–Ryan Blundell, CEO, MTG

Pete brings a unique blend of strategic thinking and deep empathy. I've recommended him to numerous CEOs because I trust his ability to create clarity and drive success. He delivers every time. If you're an Accidental CEO, this book is a must-read.

-Vern Hanzlik, CEO, VisitIQ

I sought Pete's expertise after realizing our commercial effort needed attention. Pete was able to step into our business and very quickly harmonize our marketing and sales efforts. He also engaged our operations team to promote organizational alignment in fulfilling customer needs. We continue to leverage the tools and techniques Pete developed with us.

-Mike Czop, President, Domico Med-Device

Working with Pete was invaluable as my business and our challenges changed. Pete's counsel was right on the mark. His approach gets my highest recommendation for anyone seeking to better understand how to organize their team and grow toward success.

-Sean Stevens, Owner, Home Story Visuals

Pete has a talent for turning ideas and strategy into action. He knows what leaders need to understand to make real change, and his confident, collaborative coaching style makes big tasks seem easy. This book is a must-read if you're looking for a real breakthrough in your business!

-Dave Meyer, President, BizzyWeb

Watching Pete work with his clients is inspiring. His ability to bring clarity to complex situations is unmatched. He has a gift for making the complex simple.
—Joe Cecere, CEO, Little & Company

I've had many jam sessions with Pete over the years. I keep coming back to him because he challenges me to check my biases and think past barriers. He is a hugely supportive, results-driven business partner whose influence creates clarity and purpose.
—David Novak, Board Member, CycleHealth and Craton Consulting

I trust Pete because he walks the walk. His transformative results with his clients speak for themselves.
—John Doehring, Founder and President, J. Doehring & Co.

I've had the pleasure of seeing Pete's expertise in action, and he's one of the sharpest minds when it comes to helping technical experts transition into strong business leaders. His ability to cut through complexity and bring clarity to leadership, strategy, and growth is what makes him a trusted guide for so many 'Accidental CEOs.'
—Tim Martin, CEO, FS Studio

As an executive coach dedicated to leveling up Fortune 500 leaders, I've seen firsthand the transformative power of strategic clarity—especially for up-and-coming CEOs. Pete Steege delivers this clarity in spades. His book Radical Clarity is a brilliant roadmap for CEOs and execs, blending sharp insights with a heart for authentic leadership and communication—which we need now more than ever.
      -Cindy Skalicky, Owner, On Point Communications

Pete doesn't just advise—he partners with you for strategic clarity and business acceleration. His approach is purposely meaningful, and it makes him stand out in delivering results.
      -Erika Hecht, CEO, Market Ascent

Pete is the best kind of leader. He's one of the rare ones who understands the true power of meaning and belonging for business impact and success. His results speak for themselves.
      -Jen Croneberger, Founder, Human Leadership Institute

I've had the privilege to work side by side with Pete on multiple projects in a variety of businesses, and his deep business acumen on what makes a successful company run consistently leads to real, measurable results. He quickly establishes value as a trusted advisor in every organization he works with.
      -Chad Specht, President, North Star Advisors

CONTENTS

Foreword *15*
Introduction *17*

1. The Accidental CEO 23
2. Accidental Business Challenges 35
3. Accidental Consequences 45
4. The CMP Growth Waves 55
5. Wave 1 - Uncover Your Meaning 69
6. Wave 2 - Deploy Your Meaning 83
7. Wave 3 - Scale Your Meaning 99
8. Wave 4 - Sustain Your Meaning 117
9. Radical Clarity in Action 129
10. How Accidental CEOs Get in Their Own Way 139

Your Next Steps *147*
About the Author *155*
Books by Pete Steege *157*

This book is a blueprint for technical leaders in the CEO seat to clarify their purpose, inspire their team, and grow their business. If this is you, make your experience even more valuable with worksheets, Accidental CEO profiles, additional training, and other resources at:

<u>b2b-clarity.com/resources</u>

Scan the QR code here:

Go get them now!

FOREWORD

I was skeptical when Pete Steege said he could help me grow my business. Don't get me wrong — he's a true expert on the topic. But I thought, not another business guru with quick fixes and recycled business advice. But then I worked with him personally. And here's what I found...

Pete brings a refreshingly unique approach. He goes straight to the root of the real challenges technical and accidental CEOs like me face every day. He actually looked past obvious solutions that you hear everywhere else.

If you are an Accidental CEO, Pete's approach will stop you in your tracks and make you rethink everything about how you lead, how you prioritize, and how you build momentum as you grow your technology business.

Pete helped me think clearly, act decisively, and rally my team around what truly matters. And that has made all the difference in my business.

Here's the process: First, clarify the core purpose of your business—why you exist, the unique value you deliver, and who stands to gain the most. Second, use that clarity as the bedrock for every decision and conversation inside your organization. Third, let that alignment fuel your growth, strengthen your culture, and position your company as a market leader.

It sounds simple because it is simple. But simplicity doesn't mean easy. It takes focus, commitment, and a willingness to challenge your own assumptions. I've done this work, and the impact on my business has been profound. I'm confident it will be for you, too.

Mike Loukusa

CEO, Immersion Data Solutions

INTRODUCTION

Accidental CEOs, This Is For You

Congratulations!

If you're reading this, chances are you're an Accidental Chief Executive Officer (CEO). By that, I mean you're an expert in your field, leading a business that grew out of your passion. You may have started the company yourself or taken over the reins from someone else. Either way, you didn't set out to be a CEO—but here you are. And your expertise, harnessed in your company, is making a difference in the world. More specifically, it's making a difference for your customers, your employees, your family, and for you personally.

But just because your business is functioning doesn't mean you don't have challenges. After years of working side by side with Accidental CEOs, I've found that most struggle in similar ways, almost all of which are rooted in lack of clarity. I wrote this book to help Accidental CEOs like you excel as business leaders in ways that aren't informed by your technology, your product knowledge, or your skills. Things like:

- How to engage your team
- How to attract prospects to your business
- How to become known as a market leader
- How to evolve as the business scales
- How to live a balanced life, no matter how big your company becomes

You will gain from the experiences of leaders like you who have learned new ways to engage their teams and clients. Most importantly, you will develop a rock-solid foundation for your business that will withstand changing technologies, business strategies, best practices, market conditions, competition, employees, and customers. This core building block will enable you to unify your team, accelerate your business growth, and transform yourself as a leader.

You will learn to be the CEO that you know you need to be to fulfill your vision, which I suspect is the reason you started your company in the first place.

Your New Tool: Radical Clarity

I've found that most Accidental CEOs, while naturally capable as technologists, have a blindspot or two when it comes to being the boss. Don't get me wrong, you're good at most of what it takes to be a CEO. You're good at what got you here, but 'good enough' won't achieve the big dreams you envisioned when you launched your venture.

If you're looking for a CEO 101 textbook, this isn't it. This book is more like a recipe for how adequate experts-turned-leaders can lean into their strengths while learning a new superpower for themselves and their business: the power of meaning.

You'll learn to apply my process for CEO transformation called the Clarity, Meaning, Purpose (CMP) Growth Wave. It's based on the realization that meaning is at the center of personal and commercial success but remains trapped behind a wall of complexity. Change happens when meaning is unleashed in your business through radical clarity, starting a powerful chain reaction:

- **Clarity** reveals meaning.
- **Meaning** sparks purpose.
- **Purpose** activates your business and your life.

You'll learn how to apply radical clarity to:

- Uncover your True Story
- Deploy meaning in your business
- Scale that shared meaning to become a market leader
- Sustain that valuable meaning in your company, your industry, and your family when you're finally finished with this chapter of your life.

With the CMP Growth Wave, you'll learn how clear truths matter just as much or more than capabilities. You'll learn to activate that truth by simplifying your message and your business. You'll learn a mindset and tools that help you go beyond the limitations of rational logic and see a step-function change in your team's engagement, your prospects' interest, and your business's trajectory.

> **Clarity** reveals meaning.
>
> **Meaning** sparks purpose.
>
> **Purpose** activates your business and your life.

The New You

Radical clarity doesn't happen overnight. After reading this book, you won't be a different person, but you will have a new path forward as a leader. You will have answers to important questions that define success for CEOs—some of which you didn't know were important issues before.

You will start seeing more progress toward the success you envisioned when you began this venture. You are on your way to being a more fulfilled and successful leader:

- Your team will be clear on your business's purpose and have a new urgency about their work, becoming more aligned with each other on priorities and processes.
- Your customers will understand your value better. They will see you in a new light as the provider of a unique solution that is indispensable.
- Your market will know your business and will seek you out for your deep insights and progressive innovations. Others will compare themselves to you.
- Your Finish Line, the destination you had in mind when you started on this adventure, will no longer feel out of reach. You'll have a clear plan for what's next and will know that your legacy is preserved for the good of the industry, your stakeholders, and your family.

This book is not a cure-all, but I don't think that's what you're looking for anyway. It's a toolkit for intelligent and resourceful leaders that gives you innovative ways to overcome your unique growth challenges and opportunities. You won't need all of the tools or the same tools for every challenge. But you will learn how to use them all for when the time comes.

You will gain confidence. You will be more decisive and more proactive as you make difficult decisions that no one else can make (the most important job of a CEO). You'll also make fewer of the decisions that others can make.

You will learn to be the CEO you need to be.

Don't Stand In Your Own Way

The easiest path for you is the most common path: keep on keeping on. You've achieved success throughout your career with grit: doing the work, applying your skills, and pushing through to solve the problem in front of you. Just try harder and stay committed.

From my experience, what's worked for you in the past won't work this time around. That conventional approach results in confusion, complexity, and inconsistency. The harder you try, the worse it gets.

Without a meaningful, intuitive truth to anchor and unify your mission and your business, you will continue to struggle to grow. You'll remain distracted and consumed by symptoms:

- Disagreements among your team on direction and priority that never seem to get resolved
- Too many fires to put out, distracting you from making proactive progress on your most important initiatives
- Employees who aren't committed to your vision and might leave at any time
- Apathy from your prospects and the market
- A complicated, confusing message about your offer that doesn't have traction
- Reactive changes in direction that disorient customers and slow down development
- Stunted growth as a CEO; you are not clear on your path to improve
- Continually resetting or postponing your three-year goals for the business

This book offers a new path: Instead of leaning solely on your natural skills, step back and get clear on your shared purpose, adding a new level of capability that unleashes another dimension of value—for you, for your business, and your legacy.

It's not hard to accomplish; it's just different. And sometimes, different makes all the difference.

CHAPTER #1

The Accidental CEO

Accidental CEOs are good at their job. Their businesses are robust, with aggressive goals and huge potential. Their industry peers respect them. But inside, they don't always feel that way. They wonder if they can do better.

This book is all about Accidental CEOs and how they can leverage their unique perspectives and skills to grow—their business, their team, and themselves. But first things first, let's get clear on exactly who it is we're talking about.

Are You An Accidental CEO?

I was born an engineer. I grew up with a passion for building things. I became an Electrical Engineer, and to this day, I am always in the process of building something—a business or personal project that scratches my itch to create. I am curious about almost everything.

Despite all of that, I found myself drawn to leave "the Lab" and build a career helping technology companies grow with sales, marketing, and operations. I didn't plan things to go that way; they just happened.

Today, I am the President of my own business. Being the leader of a company was not something I pictured until I did it. And yet, I have never been as passionate about my work and as satisfied with my contribution to the world as I am now. I am an Accidental CEO, and since you're reading this book, I suspect you are, too.

My definition of an Accidental CEO is a domain expert who has evolved to become the leader of a successful business. They either founded the company or moved into the CEO role because they wanted to take their expertise to the next level and create a solution to an important problem.

"Can I Do This?"

Then, one day, it hits them:

I'm the CEO now. Holy crap!

They didn't set out in their careers to be the boss. Their technical skills and their passion led them to it, and it's exactly where they feel they need to be. They accepted the opportunity willingly. But the job requires things from them beyond what their technical training provides.

Don't get me wrong—Accidental CEOs are good at their job. Their businesses are robust, with aggressive goals and huge potential. Their industry peers respect them. But inside, they don't always feel that way. They wonder if they can do better.

They see things happening in the business that they know are a problem, and their product-focused background doesn't give them the tools they need to solve them. And they often don't know what is needed to solve these challenges. Worse yet, they suspect that there are even bigger leadership issues that they are not even aware of.

> My definition of an Accidental CEO is a domain expert who has evolved to become the leader of a successful business. They either founded the company or moved into the CEO role because they wanted to take their expertise to the next level and create a solution to an important problem.

They have a big vision for what this company can be and are often frustrated that their team has lower expectations than they do for what is possible. Likewise, their customers don't appreciate the full extent of the value they can deliver. No one recognizes them for the transformative potential of their solution.

This gap between conventional expectations and the extraordinary vision of these leaders is frustrating for them. "Why can't others see what we have, how fast we can grow, and how we can change the world?" They sometimes feel like a thoroughbred yoked to the Budweiser Wagon.

Importantly, Accidental CEOs care. They are doing this for more than a paycheck. They worry about their business and their ability to lead it through these challenges. They feel the weight of responsibility for their employees and their families, their professional reputation, and the business itself—the value of bringing their vision to fruition in the world. They are risking a lot for this venture, and sometimes, it feels like they have one hand tied behind their back. At the darkest times, they doubt they can succeed.

The Many Types of Technical Expertise

The term 'domain expertise' covers a lot of ground. Accidental CEOs come in all shapes and sizes. You might have started as a software developer, a mechanical engineer, or a scientist. But you could just as easily have been a policy wonk, a university professor, or a military veteran.

The common denominator is that you are a technical expert, someone who has developed a valuable competency in your field of work. Your passion was making a difference with the "science" of your specialty, whether it was literally science or some other proficiency. What you likely did not do is set out on your career, saying, "I'm going to be a CEO someday."

Every Accidental CEO is different. We all came to the leader's seat with different backgrounds, talents, perspectives, experiences, strengths and weaknesses. You will likely relate to a lot of the characteristics I've described here, but not all of them. The 80/20 Rule applies here: I encourage you to adopt the things that make sense to you and let go of those that don't.

CEO Challenges

The Peter Principle is a classic business book. Its message is that people rise to their level of incompetence. New CEOs are vulnerable to the Peter Principle because their new role is unlike any they've experienced before. It's hard to really know what it's like to be a CEO until you are sitting in the seat.

Accidental CEOs have passed that test. They are competent leaders with viable businesses. But it often doesn't feel that way because there are significant challenges they face every day. They are ready for some of these challenges; they have experience and skills that they can bring to bear on the issue. But for many of these unintentional leaders, their backgrounds and perspectives leave them unprepared.

Growing the Business

One of the most consuming challenges for Accidental CEOs is revenue growth. How do you accelerate adoption and expand the reach of your solution? There are functional challenges to growth—Sales, Marketing, Operations, and Finance—that we'll talk about in the next chapter. To start, let's talk about broader growth pains.

Breaking out of your Network

The first chapter of your business may have been like a sailboat running in a steady breeze of business that came from your network, businesses that know you, or your team. The value of a leader's network can be a timely and precious gift for young firms. It's an important boost to your business at a fragile time in its life.

But eventually, that breeze dies. How do you get strangers to adopt? You are moving from direct, intuitive relationships to indirect, manufactured relationships. There are people, product, technology, and process questions that have to be answered.

These new relationship dynamics can be one of the more important blind spots for a technically oriented leader like yourself. If you were a seasoned operational or marketing executive, your experience would serve you well here. You need to overcome it without having been through it several times. We'll talk more about specific Sales and Marketing challenges in the next chapter. Suffice it to say, this is understandably one of the most challenging new issues for Accidental CEOs.

The Frankenstein Effect

Another vexing problem is what I call The Frankenstein Effect. As your business grows, things that are true about your business, your customers, and your market will change. Last year's plan no longer works, so you pivot.

However, Accidental CEOs can overlook the need to replace the old plan with the new plan. It takes effort for you and your team, and time is short. So you bolt the new approach on and keep going.

> You are moving from direct, intuitive relationships to indirect, manufactured relationships. There are people, product, technology, and process questions that have to be answered. These new relationship dynamics can be one of the more important blind spots for a technically oriented leader like yourself.

Over time, these bolt-ons become unwieldy. Products, plans, and marketing messages become too complex and inconsistent. Team members start making arbitrary choices. Tasks have to be completed in multiple ways and in multiple systems. Frankenstein lives!

The Frankenstein Effect gradually breaks your business. It happens so slowly, though, that nobody notices until it's a material issue that affects your agility and your ability to scale. As CEO, you have to find a way to integrate change in your business continuously.

Leading Your Team

Another common gap for Accidental CEOs relates to the people in their work lives. I'm not saying that all engineers are nerdy introverts. But I am saying that the care and feeding of relationships is one of the most important roles a CEO has, and people skills may not be the personal strength that got you this far. Creating and refining your solution may have required some of that. But the CEO role brings it front and center.

Early in your business, you may have handled this well. You built a small team of passionate, like-minded people who got along well and were mostly heading in the same direction. At some point, your team has grown. And much like the limited effect of your network in gaining customers, these natural relationships are no longer enough to align and inspire the team.

These changing dynamics lead to more disagreements that you must mediate. Team engagement starts dropping off. You no longer directly hired everyone on the team. You see people speaking and acting in situations that don't match the way you would have. All this is happening as your company continues to rapidly change. How do you keep everyone on the same page?

Personal Challenges

What's going on inside of you is arguably more challenging than everything mentioned above. For possibly the first time, the buck fully stops with you. Yes, you've had increasing responsibilities throughout your career, but never with this level of consequence for so many people. It's one of the loneliest jobs there is.

Mindset

Do you really believe that you have what it takes to do this job? Every day, you are doing things that you've never done before, and the stakes are high. You don't get a chance to practice; it's Go Time.

Every CEO faces the Impostor Syndrome. Accidental CEOs can be impacted by it more than other leaders because so much of their new primary role is in brand-new areas. They have to learn to live with incompetence and still be a confident and courageous leader.

The Maker's Lens

Another mindset issue is what I call The Maker's Lens. You became a CEO because of your vision for your solution. You knew what you could create that might make a major difference in the market. That's powerful and a key to your success. But it also can be a blindspot for you as the driver of growth in your business.

- Are you spending too much time with the product team?
- Are you too focused on how things work in the business and not focused enough on what doesn't work?
- Are you centering your messaging and sales efforts on what the product does instead of what your prospects need?
- Do you understand that less is more and that business success comes from doing fewer things better?

Living a Balanced Life

Balancing work and life is a challenge for all of us. But the CEO role can take it to a new level. Add recent societal and technological changes, and work and life become difficult to distinguish. How do you balance something that you can't even differentiate?

Added to that lack of clarity is an increased level of responsibility. If you have a family, that's a clear responsibility that hopefully you've prioritized in your career. But now you have another family: your employees, whose careers and finances depend on your business.

Staying Current

Another challenge is maintaining your technical edge. Before becoming CEO, you honed your expertise simply by doing the work every day. Now, your leadership duties pull you away from the craft, so you must deliberately carve out time to keep your skills current.

Your CEO responsibilities take you away from that focus. It can be very difficult for Accidental CEOs to no longer be the most knowledgeable one when it comes to how your products work. Your identity may be tied to that expertise. You need to adapt and grow in new areas and you need to be OK with that. Otherwise, you'll be constantly pulled in two directions.

Reaching your Finish Line

Often, when I talk with Accidental CEOs about their goals, there's a Finish Line—a milestone or destination that is driving them. It's not always front and center, but it's an important motivation that keeps them pushing forward. They may want to grow the business enough to sell it and retire. Or they want to go public. Or they want to pass the torch to a family member or colleague.

More often than not, these Accidental CEOs are frustrated. They've been running toward a Finish Line that doesn't seem to be getting any closer. They have tried different strategies and tactics but don't see material progress toward the goal.

> Before becoming CEO, you honed your expertise simply by doing the work every day. Now, your leadership duties pull you away from the craft, so you must deliberately carve out time to keep your skills current.

Ironically, some CEOs reach their Finish Line and are dealing with a different challenge. What looked like a finish line, once crossed, turns into just another waypoint. They haven't arrived at the "end" after all. What do they do now?

Being a "newbie" in the CEO seat is hard enough. What makes things worse is the impact of your unique heritage on your company. It's time to take a look at the business challenges that being an Accidental CEO can sometimes create.

CHAPTER #2

Accidental Business Challenges

These strengths and liabilities aren't just interesting facts about what it's like to be an Accidental CEO running a growing business. They have real consequences in how you lead your company and how you live your life.

What makes you unique is exactly what will drive your business forward. Lean on your strengths and perspectives—you'll succeed despite any gaps in experience.

That said, a lack of holistic clarity and proper focus can lead Accidental CEOs to run into "accidental" business problems in key areas of their companies. See if you can relate to any of the challenges in these functions of your business.

Strategy

When you were launching the business, the product/offer/solution was the impetus for everything. Without a product, you wouldn't have had any customers. Without customers, your company would have a short and painful life. At this stage, tunnel vision had value to a point. Success came through focusing on your offer.

Now that you are past that critical milestone, have you changed your mindset and priorities?

- Is the team tactically focused and near-term milestone-driven?
- Are they unclear about strategy—the end goal and the way you'll achieve it?
- Is the team unclear about priorities: what to do first, what else to do, and what not to do?
- Does the organization suffer from whiplash, with shifting plans and priorities based on changes in your offering, your business, or the market? Or a single customer?

Running a business without a clear, shared strategy is painful and limiting.

Alignment

Organizations thrive because they organize; when they do, the team has a common purpose and direction. They don't always agree on things, but overall, everyone is rowing in the same direction.

You likely want this in our organization. I hope so! Alignment enables success now and growth later. But it's common for Accidental businesses to be overly focused on today's urgent and ever-changing issues. This clouds perspective for everyone and results in misalignment, which drives conflict, confusion, and complexity.

If you doubt this is an issue, please test it: Make the rounds with your team members and individually ask them what they think is most important for the business today. Better yet, ask them what the ultimate goal of the business is. I suspect you will be surprised by how all over the map their responses are.

Sales

Sales teams generate sales (what a well-named function!), and it has to work. And the better it works, the faster you can accelerate a well-built product in a well-timed market.

Some Accidental CEOs are new to Sales or struggle to lead it. And Sales is difficult to lead. Without the proper leadership:

- Sales teams hold Marketing overly responsible for their performance (lead quantity and quality)
- The sales process can become too transactional, limiting deal size, volume, and customer lifecycle
- Salespeople overfocus on price, decreasing margins
- Compensation plans are misaligned, incenting "bad" deals that hurt the business for months or years
- CEOs are actively involved in the details of every deal. Nothing closes without them in the room
- Your team does not use the CRM system effectively, wasting a big investment and leaving the business in the dark

Without a well-managed salesforce and sales funnel, the business flounders, no matter how compelling the product or service offering is.

> It's common for Accidental businesses to be overly focused on today's urgent and ever-changing issues. This clouds perspective for everyone and results in misalignment, which drives conflict, confusion, and complexity.

Some Accidental CEOs have a sales superpower. They sold their original idea to get the business started and then sold the product itself to get the first customers in the door. They may still be the head of Sales today.

For them, this blessing may have become a curse. They are reluctant to let go of Sales as the business grows. The Sales team is frustrated and distracted from the things they need to focus on. These CEOs need to transition beyond the role of Sales Leader to fulfill their mission.

Marketing

One of my most transformational clients came to me because he needed to build a strong brand for his business but had no clue how to do it. While some Accidental CEOs don't admit it, most of them struggle with marketing. A company's brand is strongest when it is intuitive, simple to grasp, and easy to share. Clarity is the oxygen of branding.

Beyond just their brand, Marketing overall is critical for breakout success and is, at its core, about building relationships with customers. But even the best-run companies wrestle with doing this effectively. It's a challenging mix of beauty and impact, psychology and data. It's no wonder that many Accidental CEOs get stuck here.

Technical experts-turned-leaders have an additional disadvantage when it comes to this area of the business. They historically have a product- or solution-centric orientation, while the best marketing centers on the customer.

Another challenge for Accidental CEOs: the "soft" side of marketing. Marketing is an art and a science. The science side of marketing makes more sense to someone who has thrived leveraging data and science. And the product side of the business tends to be more quantifiable than other parts of the business.

The 'art' side of marketing—its ability to inspire, attract, and engage your prospects and customers—is not quantifiable in the same way. Spreadsheets are essential in marketing, but they only go so far.

Common symptoms of marketing that's missing something essential:

- Your clients mostly come from a connection with you or your team members.
- You have complicated product and market messaging that confuses your prospects.

- You depend on "inside baseball" jargon in your communications, including lots of acronyms, specifications, and product capabilities.
- Your marketing communications are ignored or, at best, met with weak engagement.
- You don't know which marketing tactics to invest in.
- Of those you do invest in, you don't know which are working.

> Beyond just their brand, Marketing overall is critical for breakout success and is, at its core, about building relationships with customers. But even the best-run companies wrestle with doing this effectively. It's a challenging mix of beauty and impact, psychology and data. It's no wonder that many Accidental CEOs get stuck here.

Marketing remains such a challenging area for businesses because there are rarely clear answers to these questions. The marketing services market provides literally thousands of activities—tactics—for you to choose from to deploy in your business. There is no one-size-fits-all combination. Every company needs a marketing plan that aligns with its products, target market, marketing maturity level, revenue, profit margin, growth plans, and more.

After years of working with Accidental CEOs to solve growth issues, I believe that marketing underperformance is one of the dirty secrets pervasive in business. They keep these shortcomings to themselves. No leader wants to admit the problem, and yet it is one of the biggest obstacles keeping them from achieving their goals.

Operations

Transitioning a business from product-focused "just get it done" startup priorities into a steady-state operational ecosystem that drives the business to achieve its long-term goals is no small feat. It's not as simple as just adding things to your priorities list. It's not solved by simply issuing directives in staff or one-to-one meetings with your leaders. This rising operational noise level is something you're likely feeling every day. You may even have lost control of the levers to success.

Symptoms of operational challenges for Accidental CEOs:

- Your team is constantly firefighting urgent issues that delay solutions to more important issues
- Your annual plan loses relevance a few months into the new year
- Projects and meetings have an overly internal focus
- Your operational meetings include a long list of metrics, most of which don't drive action in the business
- Email and messaging tools are ineffectively used and over-consumed

Accidental CEOs can overfocus on the logistics and systems of their business. Don't get me wrong—these elements are critical to your success. But when they are created and pursued without underlying alignment across the organization, they are chaotic and rarely work well.

A root cause analysis of operational failures frequently points to lack of alignment with business goals and values, where decisions and actions are not in line with where the business intended to go or what you were trying to become.

Another common operational challenge is a disconnect between internal priorities and customer needs. In the confusion of their chaotic environment, Accidental CEOs can miss the shift in their business over time away from their clients.

> Accidental CEOs can overfocus on the logistics and systems of their business. Don't get me wrong—these elements are critical to your success. But when they are created and pursued without underlying alignment across the organization, they are chaotic and rarely work well.

Early in a business's life, the customer is front and center. It's clear to everyone that without a satisfied customer, the business will die. As the company grows, two things happen:

1. New projects and priorities steadily get added to everyone's plates, which tend to distract from the focus on the customer. Early on, every other meeting was about a customer and what they needed. What share of your meetings are about client needs today?

2. The customers have less direct impact on your team. Early on, everyone knew the customers or what they needed from you. Now, there are one or two degrees of separation. A growing number of employees don't have any direct contact with clients, their expectations, or their experiences.

When left to its own devices, success becomes the distraction that pulls your business off course. Your operational challenges come in part from your inability to keep your business clearly focused on your customers.

Finance

Another area that is likely new to you is Finance, and specifically, how to fund your venture. You may have had to learn a new language and interact with a different group of people. You have had to learn how to do this well because your business's health and growth likely have depended on it.

One of the biggest challenges for Accidental CEOs here is just finding the time. Funding rounds can be all-consuming. How do you invest in this and still have time and energy to run the business?

While you were learning your trade and becoming the technical expert that you are, more traditional CEOs-in-training were learning about the world of Finance. They may even have a Finance degree or have come to the job through a career in the financial world.

Without financial experience, you have to learn on your feet. How do you decide on the best funding approach for your business, from bootstrapping to Venture Capital and everywhere in between? What kind of resources should you access to accomplish this—both inside and outside your business? How much ownership will you and your team maintain in the business?

Finally, as your company grows and these financial implications and structures have taken shape, your next decisions are much more impactful. It's no longer just about you and your family; your choices and actions affect your employees and your investors' financial futures.

These strengths and liabilities aren't just interesting facts about what it's like to be an Accidental CEO running a growing business. They have real consequences in how you lead your company and how you live your life.

CHAPTER #3

Accidental Consequences

If you continue to let outside forces drive your thoughts and actions rather than anchoring you in your mission, you are abdicating leadership of your legacy.

Accidental CEOs are a special breed. I believe their unique make-up is overall a strength that prepares them for excellence in the leader's seat. However, as we've seen, these technically oriented individuals carry some unique baggage into this job as well, with consequential effects.

What Got You Here Won't Get You There

I suspect that many of the challenges I mentioned in the last chapter resonated with you. A few of them probably were uncomfortable to acknowledge. But you might also be thinking that you can muscle through these kinks in your life and business. After all, that's worked in the past.

Here's the hard truth: this time is different. There are more dimensions and stakeholders to being a CEO than any job you've previously had. And willpower alone won't bring about the changes you, your team, and your business need to make together. You won't reach your Finish Line without an elemental change to your approach.

Stuck in the Expertise Echo

You've spent decades developing your domain expertise. These formative years have left an indelible mark. You will always be that expert deep inside. Without changing your approach, the Expertise Echo will be ringing in your mind every day, tempting you to be your best technical self, getting in the way of the people who now have that role.

The technology, formula, policy, or other solution that you brought to life in this venture is dear to your heart. After all, the solution is why you started this business! Without doing things differently, you'll continue to find the "how" work more interesting and important than the "why" work.

Muscle memory is real. Without a meaningful mindset shift, your title will say CEO, but you will continue to abdicate essential parts of the role. Progress stalls because some of the hard, squishy, and incredibly valuable work is being left for later. Or never.

If you don't transform how you think about the business, your unconscious default will remain at a level lower than you need it to be to move this venture forward. You can't succeed as the leader of your business if you're distracted.

Adrift as a Lost Leader

Without a shift in your approach, your leadership skills will stay stuck in first gear. The "people" part of your job will remain a liability. You'll muddle along with the leadership tools you've used effectively to get here, but you will continue to face headwinds with your team.

To reach your goals:

- Your team needs to believe in where you are leading them.
- To believe in where you're leading them, they need to believe in you.
- To believe in you, they need to learn to trust you.
- To trust you, they need to believe what you say.
- To believe what you say, they will watch what you do.

Without changing your approach, your actions will not earn their belief. You will be more tentative, and your vision will not be clear. This plants seeds of doubt in their minds. Without that personal clarity of vision, your actions won't be consistent. You will overreact to unexpected events. Your inconsistency will create doubts about whether you really know where the business is headed.

> As the Chief Executive Officer of your business, your job, by definition, is to make sure everything gets executed. But unless you make a shift towards clear leadership, you will continue to struggle with effective execution.

Whether you realize it or not, this "people" stuff is more important than what you sell to your clients. Without a change, the friction and lack of consensus will grow from an annoyance to an existential problem. The more success you achieve, the more pressure is placed on how people get along. Without shared meaning and strong purpose, the tension grows until the culture becomes seriously damaged or even falls apart. Much like some of the most famous musical groups (The Beatles, for example), you could "break up" in the midst of wild success.

Stuck in the Noise

As the Chief Executive Officer of your business, your job, by definition, is to make sure everything gets executed. But unless you make a shift towards clear leadership, you will continue to struggle with effective execution.

Without learning how to lead without doing, you will remain in the execution loop and stall growth. Until you learn to orient yourself as a leader first and an expert second, the experts on your team will not develop as you need them to. They will likely leave as well out of frustration.

Building your team to handle the things that aren't your strengths will be hard. You will continue to blur the line between what you need to know and what others with more knowledge and skill than you can and should contribute. You will continue breaking things that don't need breaking.

A Stalled Business

You know what's possible for your business. You can picture the breakout growth that propels you forward. But without the transformation we've talked about, you will continue to struggle with transferring the idea of what's possible into the hearts and minds of your team. Their expectations for growth won't match yours.

You will, at best, have to adjust your expectations downward as you miss key milestones. At worst, you may never grow materially beyond your current circle of clients.

Growth Remains Elusive

Without a clarified approach to your market, you will also struggle to implant your business promise into the hearts and minds of your prospects and customers. You will remain the industry's best-kept secret. You'll get tired of hearing "Why haven't I heard of you before?" from target prospects.

Without a meaningful reset, your capabilities-focused outreach will continue to underwhelm your audience. Prospect engagement will remain low, and qualified leads won't rise to the level your Sales team needs to meet their aggressive growth targets.

Your sales cycle will continue to be excruciatingly long despite your best efforts to shorten it. That's because clients won't grasp the urgency and won't gain trust in you. As a result, they won't commit quickly. Your retention rates will remain stubbornly low from a lack of buy-in in your continued value for them.

The Team Doesn't Gel

Without a shared purpose and direction for your team, you collectively aren't able to stay unified when the unexpected happens—which we know happens as a matter of course.

The chronic tension between your players—the unspoken conflicts as well as the outspoken critics—continues to be a drag on energy for the team. People spend too much time and effort overcoming the tension that could be channeled into moving the company forward.

You will continue to find yourself repeating your direction and reminding them about priorities. The team doesn't take ownership the way you need them to. Why don't they get it? Why doesn't it sink in? Your constant redirects will become tiresome.

Your staff continues to struggle to let go of the past, clinging too tightly to what worked last year while at the same getting more and more frustrated with the status quo. There's an old saying: "Change is a constant." The reality is that, yes, change is ever-present. But it's not constant; it's accelerating. Your challenge of change management will steadily grow over time.

The Window of Opportunity Starts Closing

Frustrations will grow, but more importantly, your urgency will increase because the window of opportunity you saw when you started your business is starting to close.

The clock keeps ticking on your breakout success. Every month that goes by without the needed progress towards your goal will gnaw at you. Every missed milestone will add to your worries.

You'll make adjustments to adapt to reality: postponing the launch, lowering the lead targets, and reducing the revenue projections. These resets will add up, and you'll wake up one day far behind your goals.

> There's an old saying: "Change is a constant." The reality is that, yes, change is ever-present. But it's not constant; it's accelerating. Your challenge of change management will steadily grow over time.

The bigger problem is that you're not just slowing down; you're retreating. Nothing stays constant; if you're not growing, you're declining. Over time, these compromises will force you to lower your spending and let people go—which puts you even further behind the pace you need to succeed.

Ultimately, you will find yourself frustrated with the status quo that is so short of your dream, overwhelmed with reactive tactical issues, and preoccupied with keeping the lights on.

A Stalled Life

Beyond your business, you have dreams for your life. Your best intentions for a far-off future with your family and friends won't move you closer to achieving them. Without better clarity about your path, your wishes will remain ethereal. You risk waking up one day and realizing another "window" has closed for you—your legacy. This window is much more personal and dear than any business opportunity.

You Suffer from Work-Life Vertigo

Continuing on your current "complexified" trajectory means your work and life goals will remain isolated as you muscle through your existence. You will continually juggle these competing priorities, and guess what: work will usually win. That may or may not be appealing to you now, but I expect you will regret it later.

Another set of competing priorities that will continue to challenge you: Now vs. Then. At some point, your long-term life vision may have been the impetus for your career path. It brought you to lead this business.

The life of a CEO is hard in ways that you haven't experienced before. Without some new tools, you risk making Now vs. Then an either/or proposition. Just as Work can trump Life, Now will likely beat out Then for you. And when Then comes, you will be caught unprepared. You may be able to recover some of your dreams at that point. Others will be gone forever.

You Don't Live Your Truth

Being a CEO is more than a full-time job. That makes it all the more important to enjoy what you do so you can maintain your sanity and stay motivated to drive the company forward. And the best way to enjoy every moment is to be your true self. One form of clarity is integrity—integrating all that you do with who you are.

Without reorienting your role and integrating your full self with the job, you will find that you're not all there. Leading your company will be less satisfying than you expected. You will feel a gnawing artificiality as you go through your day. You're faking it. That lack of integrity will increase your doubts and reduce your joy in life at work.

You will continue to spend too much time on things that aren't most important for you or your business. That's draining and less productive for the venture. Your team will follow suit as they look to you for inspiration. As you grow, you will be leading your team to the same misaligned choices that are hurting you.

Even worse, you risk normalizing ineffectiveness. Over time, what was frustrating may become comfortable. What felt counter to your values starts to feel normal—for you and your team.

You Don't Fulfill your Dreams

Without a new approach, you lead your business to too much "surviving in the moment." When I say in the moment, I don't mean you are practicing mindfulness—a positive, enriching habit. What I mean is that you think and act too much like there's no tomorrow. You make decisions without adequately considering how they impact your long-term future.

> Without reorienting your role and integrating your full self with the job, you will find that you're not all there. Leading your company will be less satisfying than you expected. You will feel a gnawing artificiality as you go through your day.

Without tapping into meaning, you will leave the future too much to chance. Granted, you can't control what happens decades from now, but you can make sure you're pointed that way. Without intentionally moving in the direction of your desired destination, you will find yourself drifting to another future.

If you continue to let outside forces drive your thoughts and actions rather than anchoring you in your mission, you are abdicating leadership of your legacy. Other events and people will decide where you end up. You will suddenly realize one day that you missed a chance to choose your destination. You'll make the best of the situation. It may even be better than the original plan. But it won't be your dream.

Do you want to take that chance? There's a better way. You have the opportunity to grow into your CEO role while staying true to your history, your vision, your passion, and your values. You can unlock this growth by using radical **clarity** to uncover meaning, leveraging that **meaning** to unite your team around a common **purpose**, and letting that purpose accelerate growth. The process is called **CMP Growth**.

CHAPTER #4

The CMP Growth Waves

Meaning isn't a magic ingredient, like pixie dust; it's not sprinkled on projects or people after the fact. It has to be baked in from the start and nurtured over time.

Clarity, meaning, purpose: each by itself is understood to be a positive factor for a successful business. I have found that when they are sequenced together in a way that builds one on another, transformational changes can occur. It's a powerful dynamic that you can harness to grow as a leader of a growing company.

The Solution: Ignite your Business with Shared Meaning

Every year, thousands of new business books are published. There are hundreds of accredited college and university business programs in the United States alone, each providing a thorough underpinning for how business works. I'm going to summarize them all in one word: relationships.

OK, I'm oversimplifying things to make a point. But I do believe that relationships drive business more than any other factor. For one business to buy something from another business, there has to be a relationship. At a tactical level, that's a transaction—an agreement to exchange one thing for another.

More strategically, the relationship is a commitment to a future together. All of the realized value of your solutions and the cumulative effects of the performance of your team roll up to this relationship. The more consequential the relationships that a B2B business has with its customers, the more profitable that business will be.

Shared Meaning Creates Relationships

Relationships require effort. Businesses can only afford to invest the time and money to find, develop, and commit to relationships that have a purpose for them. In other words, without shared meaning, there will be no relationship.

> Your business can't exist without relationships, and **shared meaning** is the necessary catalyst for any relationship. Shared meaning links the others' needs to what you offer them. Without a linked incentive internalized by both you and the other party, your customers won't be motivated to work with you, and your team won't be aligned with you—or each other.

Businesses that clarify and operationalize their meaning are more successful. The facts prove this out:

- **Revenue Growth:** A study by Deloitte found that purpose-driven companies witness higher market share gains and grow three times faster on average than their competitors, all while achieving higher workforce and customer satisfaction. https://www2.deloitte.com/us/en/insights/topics/marketing-and-sales-operations/global-marketing-trends.html
- **Brand Value**: According to Kantar Consulting's Purpose 2020 study, purpose-driven businesses increased brand value by 175% over 12 years, compared to a 70% growth rate for brands without a specific purpose. https://www.forbes.com/sites/afdhelaziz/2019/11/11/the-power-of-purpose-kantar-purpose-2020-study-shows-how-purposeful-brands-grow-twice-as-fast-as-their-competition/
- **Employee Productivity**: Employees with a clear sense of purpose are 50% more productive than those who are merely engaged, as reported by Bain & Company. https://www.bain.com/insights/purposeful-work-the-secret-weapon-in-the-new-war-for-talent/
- **Growth and Innovation**: Executives from purpose-driven firms are more than twice as likely to report successful transformation and innovation efforts, based on findings from Ernst & Young and Harvard Business Review. https://hbr.org/sponsored/2016/04/the-business-case-for-purpose

Despite these facts, meaning is not often a top priority for businesses. And technology-driven businesses are the most likely to de-prioritize or even ignore the "soft stuff" in favor of focusing on facts about their quality or capabilities.

- According to McKinsey, digitally savvy sectors like high tech, media, and telecom achieved a digital transformation success rate of just 26% in 2018, suggesting challenges in effectively implementing meaningful changes. https://www.mckinsey.com
- A 2021 survey revealed that nearly 75% of B2B purchasers felt that technology vendors often lack honesty, indicating a significant trust gap in the tech sector. https://www.swordandthescript.com/2022/02/b2b-tech-buyers/

A Meaningful Option

What if you were to swim against the current of complexity towards meaning? What if, instead of pushing harder and focusing on forcing results with actions, you were to use the power of purpose to pull your business and your clients forward? What if you injected meaning into everything you do as a CEO?

The first thing that would change would be inside of you. You would find yourself clearer about your motivations. You would have a stronger sense of purpose as a CEO. You would be more intentional with your time and more aware of how you live your days. You would be less reactive to unexpected events. You would care less about yourself and more about your team and your customers.

After a while, you will see changes in your team. They would care more about the business and their part in it. They would act more confidently and feel more secure about the business's plans. They would fight less and interact more in pursuit of a common purpose. They would act more consistently with clients and each other, strengthening your brand organically.

Your prospects and customers would notice the difference. Their defenses would lower. Your true value will attract more of the right prospects. Prospects would trust you sooner and more deeply. Customers would be more satisfied with your relationship. Interactions would be more collaborative and less adversarial. More of your clients would advocate for you with their peers.

Meaning is the quiet power that truly drives business success. By uncovering and applying this power, you can become the CEO you want to be and transform your company.

CMP Growth: How It Works

Meaning has proven its power to drive change in every facet of our lives, including business, over the years. But meaning isn't a magic ingredient, like pixie dust; it's not sprinkled on projects or people after the fact. It has to be baked in from the start and nurtured over time.

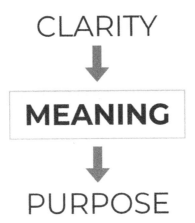

This meaningful transformation happens in three steps:

1. **Clarity Uncovers Meaning**

    In order to use meaning, you have to find it first. The chaos and hectic pace of the CEO's life in typical growing, evolving firms crowd out the core truths that are at the center of meaning for you and your business.

    The first step of CMP Growth is away from the noise. It's radical clarity. You need to take yourself out of the urgency and get a clear perspective of the bigger situation. You need context. You need the smoke to clear so you can see what's really going on.

    It's not only facts you need access to. Objectivity and subjectivity both play a role in your business—in how you see things, how your employees perceive their role, and how your customers understand their needs.

Radical clarity comes through breaking things down and simplifying the story. It comes from comparing your world to completely different industries and approaches. It takes calm courage to be open to the unexpected.

> What if you were to swim against the current of complexity towards meaning? What if, instead of pushing harder and focusing on forcing results with actions, you were to use the power of purpose to pull your business and your clients forward? What if you injected meaning into everything you do as a CEO?

When you get truly clear on your situation, the truth peeks out. By turning down the volume and clearing out the clutter, the core truth appears. It's simple and intuitive. Because everyone experiences this truth together and individually, all people get it. This discovered truth is the shared meaning that will inspire action.

2. Meaning Sparks Purpose

But meaning alone isn't personal enough. It's still an "Ivory Tower" truth that needs to be applied to work. This second step is critical—personalizing your core truth into shared meaning: purpose. It requires that everyone involved own that meaning for themselves in their own way. You need to translate meaning into purpose.

"Purpose" is everyone's "why." It holds people accountable by speaking to them in a way that they can't ignore because it aligns with their values and motivations.

3. Purpose Activates your Business and your Life

When your team internalizes purpose, they become willing to put your shared goals ahead of their individual conveniences. They will gladly push beyond what they thought they could do and discover new value for themselves. It's an empowering thing!

Your clients will be drawn to your purpose because they see that where you're going is in line with where they want to be. They are more willing to act and more willing to invest in you. They will trust you because it's not just you they are trusting; it's the bigger idea that you have shown them that is driving your business.

Meaning-activated purpose drives you, too. It anchors you in your chaotic life and guides your difficult decisions. It points you toward the CEO you want to be because when you are acting in response to your core truth, all roads lead to growth.

The Cascading Benefits of CMP Growth

This Clarity-Meaning-Purpose process—the "meaning sandwich"—isn't a one-time occurrence. It's a recurring cycle that can drive growth continuously and transform you and your business.

As an Accidental CEO, you can apply CMP Growth in waves to:

- Mature as a leader
- Position your business for faster growth
- Enable your team to gel and flourish
- Evolve your business as it scales
- Lead your market and change your industry
- Leave a lasting legacy

While CMP Growth is a tool you can apply in almost any endeavor, I've found that Accidental CEOs who implement it in four sequential waves get the most benefit for themselves and their business.

> The secret to capitalizing on the power of shared meaning in your business and your life is unity. You start with uncovering one central truth that bonds the personal You and the CEO You. From there, that same truth can expand and spread for ever-widening impact, like a pebble thrown into a quiet pond.

That said, don't limit yourself. Once you understand how it works, you can apply it in many situations across your business and your life. You'll be able to make a CMP Growth "meaning sandwich" whenever you've got an appetite for growth.

CMP Growth Waves

The secret to capitalizing on the power of shared meaning in your business and your life is unity. You start with uncovering one central truth that bonds the personal You and the CEO You. From there, that same truth can expand and spread for ever-widening impact, like a pebble thrown into a quiet pond.

CMP Growth generates waves of impact that ripple out from your true story and, from there, get deployed in every corner of your business. CMP Growth continues by washing over your customers, your market, and your industry.

Most importantly, the CMP Growth ripple effect can continue after you're gone. At some point, you'll cross your finish line, but your value and influence live on, carried by the meaning you planted, establishing your legacy of purpose and growth.

Let's peel the onion on the CMP Growth Waves. I'll provide a summary of each of the four Waves in this chapter. In the next four chapters, we'll dive deeper into each Wave and how you can activate this CMP Growth in your life.

Note that you likely have some CMP Growth Waves in motion in your business and life today. No problem! The process I'm describing will give you tools to fill in gaps and unleash new capabilities in your journey towards becoming an even more effective, purpose-driven leader and accelerating growth in your business.

Wave 1: Uncover Meaning

Wave 1 is the most important because it's where radical clarity works its magic. You need to clarify the core truth tied to your business, that is, the source of your impact and influence across all of your spheres of influence.

First, you'll take stock. You'll use The Growth Blocker Assessment and The Accidental CEO Audit to identify the strengths you bring to your role from starting as a technical leader and the gaps that you need to address. You'll slow down, get clear, and let the truth come out.

Next, you'll build your Truth Chain. That's the linkage between your business and your ideal client—the one you've built your business for. You'll construct a step-by-step connection that bridges the gap between how you see the world through your business and what your customers desperately need.

Finally, you'll arrive at your True Story. This is your truth, the shared meaning that bonds you, your team, and your customers. You'll find a way to express it such that it's meaningful to you and shareable across your outward-cascading circles of relationships.

Wave 2: Deploy Meaning

In Wave 2, you install your True Story in your business. You'll learn the Meaning Mindset, which will help you inject your meaning into your team so that it becomes a uniting purpose.

You'll apply the Map/Gap/Act process to your business to understand the exact experiences your customers need with you to succeed and what's missing today. That will determine your priority next steps to close those gaps.

Finally, you'll learn how to construct a GPS Growth Engine for your business, creating a living, breathing, steady-state ecosystem powered by your True Story.

Wave 3: Scale Meaning

In Wave 3, you build on your purpose-driven business model to lead your market. You'll apply Market Singularity and Business Physics to become the clear leader in your space.

You'll also learn to evolve as a leader of your team as the business scales. Diagnostic tools like the Impact Matrix, the Neo Organization, and Liquid Planning will help your team stay united and engaged despite rapid growth and disruptions.

Finally, you'll see how you can scale your effectiveness and maintain control of your much larger organization. You'll learn to keep the business lean and some methods to maximize your ownership.

Wave 4: Sustain Meaning

In Wave 4, you gain tools to extend your impact beyond yourself. You'll understand how to de-clutter your business with Zero Culture to maintain your team's focus on what really matters.

You'll learn how succession planning can preserve the power of purpose in your organization. Tools like Functional Reviews, Organizational Roadmaps, and The Winner's Circle will help you implement these structures.

Finally, you'll define your Finish Line. You'll get a deeper understanding of how your end goal is really just your next goal and how to plan for a succession of future Finish Lines.

Your Meaningful Future Awaits

That's a lot, I know. I believe you'll find that this process is easier than it looks. The four Waves build sequentially, and the tools we'll unpack reinforce each other. Whether you apply all of the tools or a select few, I'm sure that you'll be more confident in your role, more effective as a leader, and more successful as a business.

CHAPTER #5

Wave 1 - Uncover Your Meaning

Wave 1 helps you reveal what that shared truth is and package it in a way that communicates its meaning for everyone involved.

The first CMP Growth Wave powers the rest. The three waves that follow it ripple through your business and your life from this first "cannonball" of shared meaning. Without aligned clarity around the core truth of your business, you will continue to struggle to lead, grow, and scale.

Your business has a purpose that flows from your personal mission and values. If it weren't, you would be in this seat right now. Wave 1 helps you reveal what that shared truth is and package it in a way that communicates its meaning for everyone involved. This truth will activate the awesome power of radical clarity to propel you and your business across the remaining three Waves.

Document Your Strengths and Weaknesses

The first step in defining the truth of your business is to take stock of yourself. As an Accidental CEO, you don't fit the mold of a career business leader—and that's a good thing. Your game-changing skills and passion are what got you this far. They will continue to give you powerful advantages.

But you are lacking experience in important areas. It's easy to ignore these issues or kick them down the road to deal with later. For CMP Growth to work in your business, now is the time to face them. A clear-eyed understanding of your strengths and weaknesses as a leader is essential for you to adapt, grow, and meet the moment.

Uncover Gaps with the Growth Blocker Assessment

Dedicate some time away from your day-to-day responsibilities where you can be quiet and spend some time "off the clock." I've found that when CEOs physically remove themselves from their workspace, they have more success with this process. While there, reflect on your strengths and weaknesses with the Growth Blocker Assessment.

No matter how you came to sit in the CEO seat, you will need to play in three Arenas: Product, People, and Profit. The Growth Blocker Assessment is a structured way to document where you stand in each Arena.

The Growth Blocker Assessment

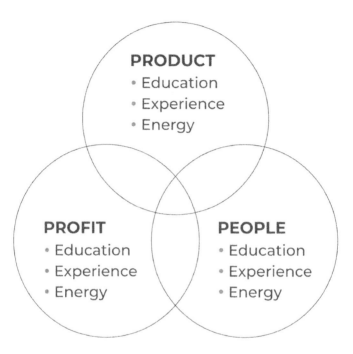

The Product Arena is where you create what your business delivers: Research, Development, Production, and whatever it takes to make the solution work for your customers. This Arena is likely where you are strongest based on the domain expertise and passion you bring to the CEO role.

The People Arena is where relationships live. It includes leading your team, building a culture, relations with customers and other stakeholders, and your family.

The Profit Arena is where the money is. It includes revenue, profit margin, valuation, growth, scaling, and exit.

The Growth Blocker Arenas don't line up cleanly with conventional business functions. Those strategic and operational structures play a role in how you run your business. We're focused here on what you bring to the business.

The Assessment Process

Picture yourself in each Arena. To get your thoughts flowing, ask yourself the following questions about how you show up in that Arena. Then, continue to capture your assessments as they lead you to what's important about where you are today.

What **education** or training have I had in this Arena?

- What degrees or certifications have I earned?
- What books and podcasts have I consumed?
- What knowledge am I missing from this Arena?

What **experience** do I have in this Arena?

- What jobs have I had with responsibilities related to this Arena?
- Was I minimally exposed to this Arena, or do I have deep experience?
- What functions or roles within this Arena am I inexperienced in?

What **energy** do I have for this Arena?

- Have I ever been drawn to this Arena in my career?
- What do I grasp easily in this domain, and what is a struggle to understand?
- Where have I been successful and where have I not?
- What have I found draining?

Reflect on what you discover. Identify key learnings, especially areas that prompt a strong reaction. This process is most valuable when you periodically revisit it and observe what's changed over time.

Go Further with the Accidental CEO Audit

For more insight on how what you bring to the CEO role affects you in your job, you can take the Accidental CEO Audit. This structured tool walks you through a series of ratings of yourself against five critical CEO outcomes: Leadership, Strategy, Growth, Alignment, and Culture. You'll get a more quantified view of where you stand and what will be most valuable to you from the rest of the book.

The power of this work is self-knowledge. Fearlessly understanding who you are and what you bring to this role will help you craft a plan to do all of these things in ways that play to your strengths. There is no right or wrong to how equipped you are for playing in each Arena.

Successful CEOs aren't strong at everything; they figure out how the team can collectively get it done.

Take the Accidental CEO Audit

Scan the QR code here:

b2b-clarity.com/accidental-ceo-audit

Mine Meaning with the Truth Chain

Now that you have an unvarnished view of yourself as a CEO, you can expand your perspective to include your business and your customers. The Truth Chain is a step-by-step exercise that helps you mine the meaning shared between all of you.

The Truth Chain is a five-link connection that brings together your business and your customer. Without doing this work, Accidental CEO-led businesses often suffer from talking past their prospects. Your prospects don't want to hear about you or your product; they want to know how you can help them solve their burning issues. The Truth Chain helps you turn your story into their story.

Conduct this exercise with your core leadership team. That's important because now we're moving beyond what's in your head.

Success from here comes from developing shared meaning. The first group that needs to unite around this is your team.

The Truth Chain

The Anchor Link: Your Business

Start at the bottom end of the Truth Chain: your business. For this anchoring link, you need to capture why your business exists and what value you bring to the world. Don't use corporate-speak; be piercingly honest about your reason for being here, what motivates you to come to work every day and fight through the challenges.

The Destination Link: Your Prospects

At the top of the chain, you identify who it is you help. It's important to be crystal clear about this. We're not talking about your total available market. Ideally, this is what I call your Bullseye Customers: the ones that are so in need of what you provide that, when they first hear about it, say, "Where have you been?" We'll talk more about your Bullseye Customers in Wave 2 when we work on your business strategy. For the Truth Chain, be as specific as you can with what you know now.

> When you complete your Truth Chain, you have a platform for consistent and comprehensive messaging that not only speaks to your customers but unifies your business. Your business strategy, planning, and execution will be simpler, more impactful, and more effective. It's very concise.

The Bridge Links: Your Offerings and What They Care About

Now that you've formed the two end links of the chain, it's time to add the links that bring you to the connection point between you and your customers.

First, add a link to your lower end by describing what your business has to offer your Bullseye Customers. What are your unique capabilities that, when combined, make you the only one who can solve their challenges in the way that you do? Shoot for three distinctive superpowers. Remember, this isn't just about your product.

Next, add a link to your top prospect link by listing what they care most about that's related to your solution. Be careful not to invent things here; you want to capture their true pain and challenges, not ones that you wish they had—the more data and observations you can use, the better.

Once you've drafted these two links, revise them as needed based on how they align. For example, you may adjust your capabilities based on where you landed on their burning issues.

The Linchpin: How You Help

Finally, build the linchpin link—the one that connects your capabilities to their most important needs. The linchpin link is how you can help them solve these issues.

This magic middle connection point is the rough draft for your True Story. It empowers you to speak to your customers in their language about the things they care about most. This pivot point functions as the anchor of your messaging, succinctly communicating both what you do and what they need.

When you complete your Truth Chain, you have a platform for consistent and comprehensive messaging that not only speaks to your customers but unifies your business. Your business strategy, planning, and execution will be simpler, more impactful, and more effective. It's very concise. That may be uncomfortable for you but remember: less is more, and radical clarity unleashes enormous power in your business.

A Truth Chain worksheet is available at
b2b-clarity.com/resources
Scan the QR code here:

Put Meaning in Motion with Your True Story

Your True Story is the meaningful "splash" that puts the CMP Growth Waves into motion.

Knowing your truth—the powerful, honest connection between what your customers need and what you do—is a huge first step in communicating with and engaging your prospects and customers. But don't stop there. You need to package this truth into a story that will serve as the script for your team and the history book for your culture as you progress through the CMP Growth Waves.

One of the current trends in business is storytelling. I am a big fan of this tool because it's been proven that humans communicate best using stories. Joseph Campbell's book *The Hero's Journey* reveals the universality of stories and their power to move people. But just any old story won't do. It needs to be your one True Story.

> Knowing your truth—the powerful, honest connection between what your customers need and what you do—is a huge first step in communicating with and engaging your prospects and customers. But don't stop there. You need to package this truth into a story that will serve as the script for your team and the history book for your culture.

It needs to be a single story because your audience is busy and doesn't listen as well or as long to you as you'd like to think they do. Your message needs to be simple, intuitive, and compelling. And it needs to be the same story everywhere. If your sales team has a different understanding of your value than your service team or your product team, these different messages will confuse your customers. The messages will cancel each other out, and later they will not remember you.

Likewise, when you change your message and priorities every six months because of your exciting new product release or in response to your competitor, you lose their attention again. About the time you are getting bored with your message, it's just starting to sink in with your prospects.

That doesn't mean you should needlessly repeat yourself; different stakeholders need different information at different points in their relationship with you. But every message should be a chapter in your one story, consistent throughout.

Fortunately, you've got the seed of your True Story in the linchpin link of your Truth Chain. Work with your leadership team to translate that nugget into a still-brief expression of how you help your target audience.

When you've got a draft, reality-check the result with these questions:

- Will Bullseye Customers understand it in five words or less?
- Does it position us as uniquely able to provide it?
- Does it generate curiosity? "Tell me more."

- Does it speak in the customers' language?
- Does it avoid talking about how we do it?

Once you've got a version you like, expand the circle. Test it with your wider team and clients. Get as much feedback now as possible; you want your True Story to stay as constant as possible.

The good news is that a well-crafted True Story stands the test of time. It will evolve, but it won't change drastically. That's a characteristic of truth that will work in your favor as you scale your business and expand your influence across the CMP Growth Waves.

CHAPTER #6

Wave 2 - Deploy Your Meaning

I'm convinced that the engaged teams powering the best businesses are enabled not by rationality or facts but by a purposeful mindset.

In Wave 1, you used radical clarity to uncover the shared meaning that has been silently driving your business and give it power. Its influence was limited because it was more a feeling than a constituted reason for your business's existence. Now that it is clearly defined, you can put it to work. In Wave 2, you'll deploy your shared meaning in your team and your business.

Infect Your Team with a Meaning Mindset

Now that you've uncovered your True Story, it's time to spread it across your team, which requires more than simply sharing the words. You need to ensure that your team internalizes the message and the meaning. You're infecting them with purpose by injecting them with shared meaning.

One of the most effective ways to embrace being a CEO is to think like one. A CEO mindset that enables a purposeful organization has three essential characteristics: authenticity, intentionality, and generosity. Accidental CEOs who are able to propagate meaning across their teams and convert it from an idea to a culture understand these traits and consistently apply them in their role.

Be Authentic

Authenticity starts with self-knowledge and then moves to business knowledge. CEOs with a purpose-driven mindset have a passion for understanding their True Story because they value the integrity and transparency it generates in the organization.

Authentic leadership doesn't have to make things up. CEOs who value authenticity build a transparent organization. Communication is faster, and employees are more responsive because they don't have to translate things into "what we are supposed to say."

Be Intentional

Intentional CEOs choose to do fewer things and do them better. They put a strategy in place before entertaining any ideas about tactics. By simplifying their scope and strategizing first, intentional CEOs model productivity and clarity for their teams. The company's intentional communications rise above the noise.

Have a reason for everything you do. You can more easily measure results when you've decided ahead of time why you are investing in each activity. Intentional leadership follows through on committed projects to completion and respects the time and resources needed to deliver them fully.

Be Generous

Adopting a meaning-filled mindset leads you organically to work for the benefit of the "other"—your teammates and your customers—and then follow through to achieve the promised result for them. The path to winning over your team to this new mission comes not through persuasion or compulsion but by example.

Having a generous approach—making it your primary motive to find ways to give to your team so they can be better—strengthens bonds and increases their willingness to follow your lead. They adopt the generosity you've modeled, which generates an organic, powerful attraction in prospects.

> Have a reason for everything you do. You can more easily measure results when you've decided ahead of time why you are investing in each activity. Intentional leadership follows through on committed projects to completion and respects the time and resources needed to deliver them fully.

You may be skeptical. You may believe this meaning mindset, even the idea that mindset matters at all in your CEO role, is not the quantifiable solution you have been looking for and, therefore, isn't for you. I can relate. I was an engineer before I was a business leader. I love data, and I am drawn to process and structure.

But after a long career in a range of companies, products, industries, and cultures, I'm convinced that the engaged teams powering the best businesses are enabled not by rationality or facts but by a purposeful mindset.

Injecting your True story into your people can't be a one-time event. It requires constant reinforcement. It also requires iteration as the business, the people, and the market evolve. You are building something bigger than a product or a revenue stream. You are building a culture. That culture expresses itself as a brand, which creates goodwill and revenue over time. There are no shortcuts; you have to plant the seeds of meaning and water them with a CEO mindset to harvest the ultimate results you are working so hard to achieve.

Once you've aligned your team with shared meaning, you can move on to the other important stakeholders: your prospects and customers.

Inspect Your Business with the Map/Gap/Act Process

You have a relationship with your customers today, but is it aligned with your True Story? It's time to do a systematic review to determine what's working and what needs to be changed.

Map Your Bullseye Customer's Journey

With your True Story in mind, document your customer's ideal experience starting from before they knew who you were and sequentially on through to their becoming aware of you, seeking to learn more about your solution, committing to buy from you, using your product, buying again, and finally to the point where they are a long-time customer that tells others how great you are.

I use a seven-stage customer journey model, But there are many variations—feel free to use whatever model helps you and your team best describe your Bullseye Customer's ideal experience.

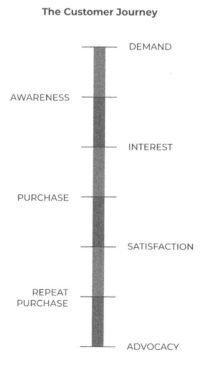

The Customer Journey

Document every detail you can about what this ideal journey looks like. Consider:

- What are they thinking and feeling before each step?
- What do they hear, see, or do that incites them to move on to the next stage?
- Who (inside and outside your business) says or does what to create that experience?
- What are the specific actions your customers take that you can observe that signals progression to the next stage?

This ideal journey paints your best future, and if you can create this experience for your Bullseye Customers, you will win them as clients. Over time, your reputation will expand to win prospects farther and farther outside your Bullseye.

Spend as much time as you need to describe this ideal sequence in detail. You'll have to make some assumptions, but that's okay. The process of envisioning your ideal customer journey is more important than how accurate it is; any level of new clarity around this path will raise critical questions for your team. You will get much more familiar with your customers and learn how you can help them.

Identify Gaps in the Journey

Mapping Customer Journeys is not an uncommon practice. You may have done this in the past. What makes this process valuable is what you do next: compare this ideal future to today's reality.

Seeing all of the gaps in your customers' path to value with you in one view gives you the perspective you need to prioritize the investment of your time, money, and attention to correct them. And you need to choose because you can't tackle all of your challenges at once.

That perfect journey is not what your customers are experiencing now. Go through the customer journey again, this time taking stock of what's actually occurring—document in detail how and where today's experience falls short. Understand the gap at each stage, where there is friction, blockage, or confusion. Are they distracted, frustrated, bored? Checked out? Where do they exit the journey? Do they skip a step?

Act First on the Most Pressing Gaps

Seeing all of the gaps in your customers' path to value with you in one view gives you the perspective you need to prioritize the investment of your time, money, and attention to correct them. And you need to choose because you can't tackle all of your challenges at once. That leads to ineffective overload and paralysis—it generates lots of activity in your business but very little progress towards your goals.

Quantify the size of the challenges at each stage:

- Where will it take the biggest change in product, customer experience, and team behavior for you to close the gap and move the customer to the next stage?

- Which stages are in good shape, close to your ideal?
- Which stages are subpar and will require significant effort to improve?
- Which stages are critically dysfunctional and not working at all?

Now, rank the gaps. These gaps become your list of business priorities for rapid growth. When your "bullseye customer journey" is built on your True Story and works as planned, your business accelerates.

Map/Gap/Act Process worksheets are available at

b2b-clarity.com/resources

Scan QR code here:

Far too often, teams view customer journeys as marketing tools. Don't think that small: you're mapping your whole operation. These aren't just sales or marketing problems. Turn to the GPS Growth Engine to close gaps across all functions.

Invest for Growth with the GPS Growth Engine

One of the most significant reasons Accidental CEOs struggle to grow their businesses is that they are trying to do too much. It shouldn't surprise you. This "overload" problem is endemic to our world. Your prospects are too busy to pay attention to you. Personally, most of us struggle with too many responsibilities, too many commitments, and too much media to consume. Likewise, your employees most likely have too much on their plate to effectively deliver, and your business has too many "priorities" to prioritize. The dirty secret of business is the painfully low success rate of programs in every department.

The Goals, Programs, Systems Growth Engine (GPS Growth Engine) applies radical clarity to focus your business on what's most important: delivering on the promise of your True Story. This focus is absolutely critical to your growth.

Distractions from your core mission slow down your progress in several ways. There's the opportunity cost of spending precious time and money on things that don't bring your customers closer to your ideal experience for them. Perhaps even more important is that new products, features, or campaigns that aren't aligned are destructive interference with your prospects and employees—they cancel out progress by increasing complexity, adding redundancy, or sending inconsistent messages.

The GPS Growth Engine is a simple way to reimagine your business with a lens towards focus, simplicity, and value. Like its namesake, the Global Positioning System, The GPS Growth

Engine orients your business and helps you get where you're going faster and more directly.

The process is simple. When I build GPS Growth Engines with my clients, it may take several months to activate their Engine's full value. The good news is that you can gain a lot even with a first-pass application from what you learn here. Dedicate a few hours over a week or two and work through the three steps of the Engine for your business. I recommend doing it "virtually" this first time without applying it to the business.

Even this relatively minor effort will give you a new perspective on your business and higher visibility into what's most important for your venture. You'll identify key opportunities and unearth some hidden challenges that are blocking your path to success. Whether or not you commit to implementing the GPS Growth Engine fully in your business, you will have an incrementally more aligned and purposeful business ecosystem than what you have now.

The GPS Growth Engine

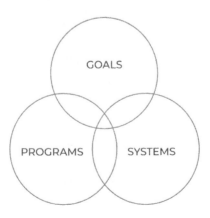

Goals: Decide on Outcomes and Plan to Achieve Them

In the Goals phase, you set a clear direction for how you will win. It's about actualizing your True Story in the simplest, most direct way possible. What's the most direct way to achieve it?

Positioning: What is it that only we can do?

Positioning makes or breaks your business. In the book *Play Bigger*, Christopher Lochhead explains how designing a market category to fit your business can position you as the best (really, only) solution for your bullseye customer's most urgent problem. If you are one of many solutions for them, it will be magnitudes harder for you to be found and engaged than if they see you as the only solution.

Targeting: Who exactly will we do it for, and when?

You've laid the foundation for your target with your True Story; now it's time to quantify and right-size it. The goal is to identify exactly who you will be engaging with. The best case is a literal list of target clients. However, such narrow targeting often doesn't work in B2C markets where success can mean selling to tens of thousands or millions of customers. In B2B, you have more ability to scale your business with a tightly defined target list or segment. You can expand wider or to other markets later; the first priority is traction in your sweet spot.

Reality check your defined target. What would winning one percent do? Ten percent? Twenty-five percent? You won't win them all right away, but it's realistic for you to be a market leader in your chosen space within a few years, given your positioning.

> A common mistake for Accidental CEOs is marketing your products as if you are a consumer company. If you have a sharply focused target market (and even a defined list of target accounts), broad-based promotion and outreach tactics have low ROI. In this situation, Account-Based Marketing and other strategic account-selling approaches are more focused and can be incredibly productive.

Strategy: How exactly will we accomplish that?

The answer to this is your scaling strategy—how you will engage with the market to win your desired number of bullseye customers in the time frame you have set. Again, it's not about how much you do but how focused you are on the right programs. Rather than adding a product, can you combine two into a just-right offer? Rather than "going wide" with your sales and marketing, can you zero in on your target prospects with a remarkable offer that they can't ignore? Commit to less, commit to doing it well, and commit to following through with measurable results; rinse and repeat.

Programs: Focus the Business on the Most Impactful Initiatives

Now that you've clarified your focus, your destination, and your approach, it's time to do the work. Of course, your team is doing lots of work already. But are they doing the right things? Are they doing the right number of things? And are they learning from the things they are doing?

Purpose-driven programs

The first step to success here is in curation. Actively choose the things your business invests in rather than letting them choose you.

That means requiring that every initiative your business invests in has a reason for existing. Make that a part of your planning process. If that reason doesn't directly support filling your priority customer journey gaps, make that clear and agree that it's worth the distraction. The same logic applies to extending existing projects. "We did it last year" is not a valid reason for investing this year. Force the team to view every investment as an opportunity cost since saying yes to something always means saying no to other things.

MVP: Minimum Viable Programs

The second key to successful programs is to leverage the Minimum Viable Product (MVP) concept made famous in the Agile Methodology for software development beyond your product development for every operational project. The general idea works just as well for launching marketing campaigns and deploying Enterprise Resource Planning platforms (ERP platforms) as it does for developing products.

These Minimum Viable Programs allow you to start small, get to usage (and feedback) sooner, and ramp up intelligently as you find your groove with any program. The users will vary from employees to partners to customers, but the process works just as well.

Measure everything

If you are investing time and money in a program, you need to know if it's working. Without that visibility, you'll end up with underperforming, suboptimal, or unnecessary programs cluttering your business. You'll also miss opportunities that come out of the insights you gain from watching and listening to what's actually happening.

Measurement sometimes gets a bad rap in business. That comes from misapplication: overcomplicated dashboards, meaningless measures that don't drive action, and "cosmetrics": vanity metrics that help people feel good but don't help the business improve.

Here are some measurement best practices that will help you implement a 100% closed loop in your firm:

- **Define success before "hiring" the project.** You need to know what you're expecting to know if you achieved it. Do this before you choose your tactic.
- **Choose one priority metric per project.** Keep it simple—agree on a single metric that determines success.

- **Size the measurement to the task.** Lower-value projects shouldn't take extensive effort to prove that they're working.
- **Be creative.** Some of the best measurements are manual—observing prospect behavior changes from a marketing campaign, for example.

Systems: Establish Simple and Scalable Processes

The final "gear" in your GPS Growth Engine is your Systems: putting the steady-state processes in place that automate repetitive tasks, maintain consistency, and enable the organization to grow efficiently. These combinations of people, platforms, and processes, executed well, will make your organization more agile and more scalable.

Simple it up

One of Seth Godin's philosophies is: "Start with basic principles, go slow and build. No need to dumb it down. Simple it up instead." These principles apply to your systems: rather than trying to remove complexity from your current system, consider how you can build it simpler from the start. The MVP concept above is a version of this.

> My favorite example of "simpling things up" in a business is using Customer Relationship Management (CRM) platforms. For decades, CRMs equated to complexity. The cost of installing one in your business could start at well over $100,000. A new generation of

> CRM platforms like HubSpot has revolutionized this process. Now, you can implement your CRM MVP with a very capable free version and incrementally evolve your process. These platforms are designed for simpling up.

Curate your business processes the same way to manage your project load, and choose your metrics. What's necessary versus comfortable—or safe? Fewer processes done well are almost always better than a lazy collection of more.

The GPS Growth Engine purrs when it is simple and adaptable. Success comes from saying no as much as from saying yes. Will your business be 100% focused on these priorities? In a perfect world, yes—but your business resides in the real world. There will always be distractions; the GPS Growth Engine will reduce the number and intensity of them and increase the time and effort spent where it matters most.

CHAPTER #7

Wave 3 - Scale Your Meaning

While you aren't fully in control of your destiny, there are ways to increase your influence over your business's direction to continue to stand tall on the larger stage you're playing on.

In Wave 2, we installed your shared meaning—your True Story—into the hearts and minds of your team and the inner workings of your business. Hopefully, you're on the path to building a CMP Growth Engine fueled by your powerful purpose. The next step: put your potent, clear truth in motion to lead your market, lead your team, and own your future.

Lead Your Market

It's time to expand your truth outward beyond the walls of your business to attain market leadership. That may sound presumptuous, but I believe that any company with a strong True Story can own its market. Here are three steps you can take to start your market-conquering mission.

Market Singularity: Be the Only One That Can Do What You Do

In Al Reis and Jack Trout's The 22 Immutable Laws of Marketing, Law 2 is:

> *If you can't be first in a category, set up a new category you can be first in.*

That insight captures the magic of the positioning exercise from Chapter 6: by claiming a unique position in your target space, you can be the leader of your market. I call this Market Singularity. Revisit your positioning and targeting results from the last chapter. If you led this market segment, would it provide you with the revenue and growth rate you need to take you to the next level? That's all you need at this point; more growth becomes available when you apply and re-apply this exercise.

If this segment is big enough to scale your business to the next level, you're in great shape. Lean into this niche with all your might. Craft a deeper story about how you uniquely solve problems here. It's time to go deeper and be specific. Explore and expand the products, features, and services that make this real. Collect direct customer feedback to validate your assumptions and spark new ideas.

If not, you need to make adjustments. Explore adjacent spaces and adjustments to your bullseye customer definition. It's critical to lock on to your strategic segment before going any further.

The Physics of Business: How Universal Principles Help You Grow

Another way to expand your business beyond your current capabilities and expectations is to leverage the power of nature—in this case, the Laws of Business: Friction, Attraction, and Gravity. Business dynamics have their own core truths, which you can leverage when you understand how they affect your interactions in the market. Let the universe apply force in ways that go beyond what you can control.

Gravity

There is an ever-present pressure on your clients: the consequences and fears of their unsolved problems. When you are focused on your bullseye customers and are able to fill the gap between what they need and what they want to achieve, that gravity takes effect. They will start to find you rather than be found by you. Look for ways to expose the truth about the gap between their pain and your solution, and let this force of gravity work for you.

Friction

Friction is another ever-present force in nature and business. Rather than accept it, your opportunity is to reduce friction in your company's processes, people, and prospects.

Simplifying your message, your process, and your solution will accelerate adoption, revenue growth, and your profitability. Reducing friction is just as valuable with your team. Helping your team interact with each other and with prospects in a more streamlined, simple, and intuitive way is going to improve your business measurably.

> There is an ever-present pressure on your clients: the consequences and fears of their unsolved problems. When you are focused on your bullseye customers and are able to fill the gap between what they need and what they want to achieve, that gravity takes effect. They will start to find you rather than be found by you.

However, there is a flipside to friction; it can also be a strategic advantage. Look at the most challenging parts of your business—the difficult technical and operational nuances that you face. If it's hard for you, it's likely hard for others. When you see friction in your efforts, consider leaning in. It may be a signal of sustainable advantage.

Similarly, friction can be an asset in customer acquisition. Suppose your lead funnel works smoothly for your best prospects but is difficult and unattractive for unqualified prospects. In that case, you save your team significant time and effort by not having to invest in relationships that won't, in the end, help either party.

Magnetism

Magnetism is the magic that draws your most profitable prospects to your business and your most valuable employees to join your team. Magnetism comes from meaning in business—your True Story. You might talk about your brand strength or product-market fit in similar ways; these concepts are all related to this natural attraction. If you activate meaning and purpose in your company the way I've described, you won't have to spend as much effort pulling; meaningful magnetism will do some of the heavy lifting.

Thought Leadership: Lead the Market Before You're a Market Leader

Idea Marketing

Thought leadership is an overused term that can mean different things to different people. It's a close cousin to marketing since it strengthens your relationship with your audience. But it's much more than a marketing strategy. It's a powerful vehicle for activating the magnetism of your brand by talking first about your customers and solutions to their problems instead of focusing your content on what you do.

What Accidental CEOs sometimes miss is that thought leadership is the most powerful pre-emption tool you have. It's kind of like "fake it till you make it"—you can paint a picture of the positive future your business will bring to the industry or certain kinds of businesses before you've fully delivered it. Use the power of that vision to draw prospects and partners into your orbit. They become fans of the future you own because you were the first to describe it.

Build a Movement

Thought leadership applies just as powerfully to your employees as it does to your prospects. Leading your team includes sharing your expertise, expectations, and aspirations for the company. Painting that picture for them will inspire them to follow you to that bright future and to stick with you through challenging times. This kind of leadership is more empowering than telling them what to do. With proper inspiration, they will stay aligned even when no one is looking.

> What Accidental CEOs sometimes miss is that thought leadership is the most powerful pre-emption tool you have. It's kind of like "fake it till you make it"—you can paint a picture of the positive future your business will bring to the industry or certain kinds of businesses before you've fully delivered it.

You're building a movement that will align and empower your team, your customers, and your partners. This movement is the kind of news and information that industry publications write about and podcasts spread over. Channels that won't talk about your products become eager to share your ideas related to the positive change you are bringing about.

Activate your Advocates

The very best salesperson for your business is not on your sales team. It is the customer who goes out of their way to tell other businesses about how great you are and shares the benefits of what you do for them. Nurture these advocates to accelerate your customer journey and grow revenue:

- Make a short list of your most active advocates—those who are talking about you with other businesses.
- Invest time in understanding what's driving them to do this. It's often not directly about your business, by the way.
- Figure out how you can help them achieve the personal goals and business goals driving their support of you, which may be more about removing friction than adding incentives.

Just a few activated advocates will make a mark in your market by spreading the good news about how you can help—which is more viral than how your product works.

Lead Your Team

As the CEO of a growing business, you are likely familiar with the "unraveling" problem—the increasing number of conflicts and fractures amongst your team as you grow that seem to come out of nowhere. Your tight squad of ten employees suddenly starts bickering when you add a few more people; your orderly team of 50 employees splinters, with conflicting agendas preventing forward motion; your stable organization of 100 staff disengages.

An organization that operates smoothly at one scale will discombobulate at some point as it grows. You need to find a new rhythm and reset equilibrium to move forward. Your shared meaning can be a potent adhesive to realign your team. Here are three tools to help you preserve alignment and purpose as your business grows.

Scale Decision-Making with the Impact Matrix

When your business was small, you made most of the consequential decisions. As you grow, you need to delegate decisions increasingly—but without the organization descending into chaos. The Impact Matrix will help you balance empowerment and control.

> An organization that operates smoothly at one scale will discombobulate at some point as it grows. You need to find a new rhythm and reset equilibrium to move forward. Your shared meaning can be a potent adhesive to realign your team.

You need to enable your team to take ownership and be accountable for their part of the mission. It's so easy for them to defer to you, and that doesn't scale. At the same time, you still need to lead the company and make important decisions. Your most motivated employees will get frustrated without a voice in this.

Empowerment and control don't have to be mutually exclusive. You can actually have the best of both worlds for an effective, high-performing organization.

- If people don't feel empowered and you're not making directional decisions, they will become **paralyzed**. There's no direction, and they aren't empowered to make things happen.
- If they're not empowered and you are making all the decisions, they end up **dependent**—waiting for orders.
- If you empower your employees in a strongly decentralized decision-making structure, you struggle to keep everybody going in the same direction—or even in the same general direction. The environment becomes **chaotic**, generating conflict and confusion.
- The ultimate win is when you can empower your team and give them accountability within a framework of tiered decision-making. Individuals own decisions that increase in importance with their responsibility, laddering up to you as the CEO and finding the right balance results in a **high-performing** environment where decisions are made without undue noise and conflict. Those decisions align as they rise in significance to the decisions you still make as your organization's leader.

The Impact Matrix

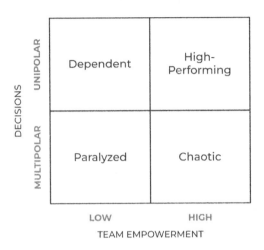

Use the Impact Matrix to understand how decisions are made today by mapping your top recurring decisions on this matrix. You might be surprised at which quadrant is your center of gravity. Use what you learned and work with your leadership team to make adjustments.

This tool has additional value: transparency. Often, you and your team members aren't clear on who owns decisions. By building out your Impact Matrix together, you gain consensus, which reduces misunderstandings and resentments as well.

Impact Matrix worksheets are available at

b2b-clarity.com/resources

Scan the QR code here:

Broaden Your Definition of Staff with the Neo Organization

Ditch the traditional view of your organization chart. In today's world, your team is made up of not one but three kinds of staff members:

- Internal Staff: your employees on the payroll
- External Staff: vendors, contractors, and freelance workers
- Cyber Staff: AI automation, bots, and agents.

External Staff are a more valid option for some work than in the past. New systems and services reduce the risk and simplify the integration of these people into your workflow.

AI-powered work is a reality going forward. No, Cyber Staff aren't people, but their contributions will increasingly equate to roles in your organization. The sooner you engage with this new resource, the faster your organization will rise on the AI adoption and learning curves, and the more valuable (and appropriate) the AI contributions will be.

Integrate all three of these worker classes into your planning. I've found that organization charts, including all three classes of workers, provide a much clearer picture for everyone of how work gets done and reveal opportunities to scale the organization in new ways. But don't stop there. Carry this model throughout your People function. You should include all three categories in your personnel planning, training and development process, and succession planning.

Shorten your Business Plan Horizon with Liquid Planning

There is a growing disconnect between the static nature of business planning practices and the dynamic reality your business lives in. Free yourself from the restrictions of conventional business planning cycles. I don't mean for you to stop planning or even to stop planning in a structured way. What I suggest is that you adapt your planning for a more fluid world.

You still need a long-term perspective on your business; I believe your three-year view is one of the most important for your business because it encompasses the time you need to make substantial changes in your business.

Annual plans have a functional role in budgeting, hiring, and major initiatives. Quarterly plans are the best for operational focus and accountability. In some environments, weekly or daily standups drive progress and keep the business nimble.

Liquid Planning is based on the idea that there is not a single timeframe, system, or business plan that is right for every company. Moreover, the best planning process for your business today likely won't work for you when you are three times as big, nor in five years when change has accelerated even more.

Plan your planning; acknowledge that this is not a constant and make it part of your strategic planning process. Continue to question the timeframe and structure of your decision-making and review processes. The rest of your business is in a state of constant flux. Why wouldn't your planning process be the same?

Own Your Future

As your business scales, so too do the forces pressing on your organization from every direction. Decisions that used to be fully in your control require collaboration and are much more consequential. Opportunities present themselves that take much more effort to exploit. The success or failure of initiatives has a much larger impact on your team, your customers, and your bottom line. The reality of your job is that you don't grow your way above your challenges; they grow with you.

While you aren't fully in control of your destiny, there are ways to increase your influence over your business's direction to continue to stand tall on the larger stage you're playing on.

Continue to Grow Personally with a Scaling Mindset

The fact that you're sitting in the CEO seat means that you likely already know what I'm about to share with you: success requires that you have a growth mindset, as Dr. Carol Dweck described in her excellent book *Mindset*. Think back to your years in the technical trenches. The challenges you faced in that role consumed you. And you outgrew them. This need to grow through today's battle to the next one will be a constant in your career and your life.

In case you think you've "arrived" as a CEO, it's time for an attitude change. You have much to learn. Your growth will be tied to scaling. Take on a Scaling Mindset, applying the growth mindset philosophy to not only yourself but your business. Part of your leadership mission is to instill this same approach within the minds of your team. Your success depends on it.

First, I recommend reading *Mindset* if you haven't. You could even use the book with your leadership team as a team-building training exercise. Consider doing it with a train-the-trainer approach so that they can do the same with their team. The growth mindset is a simple, intuitive idea that you can transfer across your organization. It mixes well with the concepts of the CMP Growth Waves.

Maximize Ownership with Customer Capital

How much ownership do you want to maintain in your business? Many CEOs assume that outside investment is the only path to growth and scale. While that is a proven method to ramp up a business, there are other options. In particular, I encourage you to consider an alternative to venture capital: customer capital.

> In case you think you've "arrived" as a CEO, it's time for an attitude change. You have much to learn. Your growth will be tied to scaling. Take on a Scaling Mindset, applying the growth mindset philosophy to not only yourself but your business.

Another word for this is bootstrapping. You use your current revenue to drive your growth. The obvious benefits: at the end of the day, you have full ownership of your business. I have two recent clients—seven-figure and eight-figure businesses, both growing at a hundred percent a year. Their businesses are profitable, and these leaders have majority or sole ownership of their companies. There's not a venture capital role in either of their businesses so far.

So, what does it take to activate customer capital in your business successfully?

'Soft' Product

Your product likely needs to be a "soft" product with little to no physical manufacturing involved. Examples are SaaS or other services companies. You can get to market with a much lower upfront investment. It will still require considerable planning and business model design to manage cash flows through rapid growth.

Tight product-market fit

You need a strong and focused product-market fit that flows operationally out of your True Story from Wave 1. You need a very tight definition of who exactly benefits most from your product and exactly how. They say, "This is exactly what we need". This alignment allows you to get to revenue faster, with less upfront cash burn.

Sustainable differentiation

Sustainable differentiation refers to the strength of your positioning from Wave 2: You need to be the only one who does what you do in your space. The two clients I mentioned are the only alternatives for their clients. Sustainable differentiation buys you time. You don't have to ramp as fast or invest as much for that growth because your opportunity window stays open longer.

Customer capital is not for every leader, but it's a practical way to maintain more ownership in your business. Also, it doesn't have to be a binary choice. The more customer cash flows that can support your growth, the less outside investment you will require and the more ownership you can maintain.

With Wave 3, you've converted ideas into progress. You stand out in your market with a crystal clear, truly unique identity. Your prospects are coming to you rather than you having to force yourself on them. Your organization is stable despite living in a dynamic environment and leaning forward. You and your business are in a much better position to grow.

But don't stop here. At some point, you will finish with this venture, this chapter of your life. What happens to all of this progress, then? It's time to talk about preserving the value you've created—your legacy—after you've won the race.

CHAPTER #8

Wave 4 - Sustain Your Meaning

Your ultimate job is to transplant your purpose into others so that it continues without you, in whatever form that takes.

You are clear on your mission and direction, and they are "true", and connected directly to your passion and purpose. You've embedded them in your team, so they own them as much as you. And you've aligned your business with this energy so that your customers and your market experience your value. You're scaling! But you're not done.

What does "done" mean, anyway? Will you stay in the business as it moves forward, continuing to evolve your own skills and value in parallel? Will you pass the torch to a new leader and steward them as they grow into the leader the business needs next? Or is the mission complete, and time for an exit?

Whatever your end game, it's not really the end. Ultimately, your success lies in how the value you created lives on. What sustains the company's purpose after you're gone? Radical clarity is the answer here as well.

Install Meaning in Your Culture for the Long Term

Many amazing companies die slow deaths when their meaning-filled leader leaves. You will leave someday, too. Even if you stay "for the duration," 50 years from now, you will most likely be gone.

To build a culture that will miss you but won't be missing when you're gone is counterintuitive. The most sustainable culture is one that's not about you (or your employees) at all. It's called Zero Culture.

Remove Customer Barriers with Zero Culture

First, let's be clear: your business will never attain Zero Culture. But, the act of working towards it as a goal will enable your business operations to continue independently of you or any other person. The firm will be able to function fruitfully, no matter who becomes the next leader or owner. It transcends time because it transcends you by focusing everything on the customer and their value.

Zero Culture is the idea that your business's purpose is to deliver on your True Story, which is ultimately about your customers getting value from you. Success comes through pursuing everything that delivers on that promise and eliminating everything that doesn't. While no company ever achieves Zero

Culture, the pursuit of it will sustain your business long after you are gone.

> Zero Culture: Find your truth and get out of the way.

Zero Ego: It's Not About Us

As I mentioned earlier, Accidental CEOs are tempted to focus on what they make versus what their customer receives. Zero Culture businesses spend more time talking about their customers and their needs than the intricacies of their technology or internal priorities. They speak using the same vocabulary as their clients. They discuss how to charge less or offer more rather than how to charge more or offer less.

Zero Friction: Get Out of the Way

Customer friction is real. It can kill your business. At the other extreme, frictionless customer journeys are magic. Zero Culture businesses relentlessly seek out and remove whatever is getting in the way of delivering value. This approach goes way beyond the sales or marketing functions to how products are built, how clients are supported, and how internal processes function.

Zero Overhead: Less Is More

Businesses suffer more from excess than scarcity. Zero Culture is about saying no to all but the best options—product features, marketing tactics, business platforms, and communication channels. Do less and do it really well. Scarcity fuels innovation, and fewer initiatives will have a much higher success rate.

Zero Delay: The Time Is Now

The rate of change is a challenge for businesses today, and the rate is increasing. Zero Culture companies root out delays in every aspect of their business. Processes are made simpler, meetings are compressed (or eliminated), and responses become less packaged. The Agile Methodology applied to every part of the business will allow you to keep up with your customers' changing needs.

Zero Culture is not a destination; it's a long-term target that will continue to motivate your organization and sustain your impact beyond you.

Succession Planning

While your business may have started with your ideas and your passion, it will survive and thrive with your people. Your reliance on your team grows stronger the bigger you scale. Your ultimate job is to transplant your purpose into others so that it continues without you, in whatever form that takes.

Succession planning is vital to making this happen. The annals of business history are full of organizations that failed not long after a longtime leader exited the firm without adequately preparing their team for their departure. Accidental CEOs who succeed are the ones who put their business above themselves and plan first to become redundant and then unnecessary.

Don't wait until you've decided on your Finish Line—your milestone for moving on from this venture. The most effective way to plan for succession is to bake it into your standard business processes. Here are three changes you can make to your business today that will help the organization be ready for life without you.

Fill the Feedback Gap with Functional Performance Reviews

Whether you call it Human Resources or your People Department, this vital function focuses on enabling and optimizing your employees. And while most businesses actively work to develop their workers, they underfocus on how the team works as a whole. This lack of team-level perspective clouds your view of how your business really works and how that needs to change over time.

> The annals of business history are full of organizations that failed not long after a longtime leader exited the firm without adequately preparing their team for their departure. Accidental CEOs who succeed are the ones who put their business above themselves and plan first to become redundant and then unnecessary.

Employees are the foundation of your business, but how they work together to deliver results is where one plus one can equal three, four, or more. Functional Reviews focus on creating more clarity in your organization by evaluating the functions of your business in the same way you evaluate individuals. Such reviews are critical since people will come and go, and your core functions need to perform steadily regardless of those changes—yet few businesses do this well or at all.

Don't confuse this with culture and personality testing that, while valuable, focuses on helping individuals work well with each other. Functional Performance Reviews address the strengths, weaknesses, and opportunities for growth of the group as a unit. Did the team meet its goals? What can the team focus on together to improve? What is the growth path for this team in the business?

Work with your People leader to make Functional Performance Reviews part of your standard People development process.

Strategically Plan for Your People with an Organizational Roadmap

Another clarifying tweak to standard business planning practices is to forecast your organization with the same focus and precision you apply to your product's future: create an Organizational Roadmap for your business.

Your Organizational Roadmap should answer the same questions you and your customers have about the future of your product or service, but about your team: What capabilities will we add over the next year? What processes and platforms are needed to make that possible, and when? How about over the next three years? How will we roll out these changes? What's our timeline for phasing out outdated roles and capabilities? How will we manage that transition internally and externally?

Your Organizational Roadmap is bigger than a staffing plan. It holistically addresses the people, processes, and infrastructure your business will employ, with corresponding plotting of the associated outcomes. It will include the Neo Organizational factors of Internal, External, and Cyber Staffing. By taking this high-level people planning approach, you prevent overfocusing on individuals and not focusing enough on the organization's success. That approach doesn't replace conventional individual personal development.

Visualize your Winner's Circle

Another exercise that will add clarity to your planning role is the Winner's Circle. The Winner's Circle exercise helps you think ahead about your final chapter in this business, your Finish Line, and align your personnel decisions with that vision.

The Winner's Circle is the team you have in place when you get to your Finish Line. We'll talk more about the Finish Line in the next section. Whatever that point in time looks like for you, it happens with the help of others. And the business continues after the Finish Line with the team that remains.

Take some time to picture yourself at the end of the "race," when you have reached your defined goal and your next chapter is beginning. Who is in the room with you? Who do you thank for helping to make it happen? What did they do to help bring the vision to reality? Paint this picture with as much detail as possible. This Winner's Circle visualization will plant seeds for you that will pay dividends now as you make staffing decisions, nurture your team, and respond to unexpected challenges and opportunities. It also makes arriving at the Finish Line less jolting for everyone; there are fewer surprises.

The Finish Line

At some point, you will arrive at your Finish Line. It might be going public, selling the business, or handing the reins to the next generation of leaders. Whatever your meaningful milestone is, how you apply this future goal today makes a huge difference.

What is your Finish Line?

Do you have a Finish Line? I hope so.

Just as effective business leaders put strategy before tactics, traversing your journey as a CEO with a specific end in mind will serve you well. Knowing where you plan to go fuels intention in your daily life and gives you a perspective that will improve your decision-making.

There's no right or wrong Finish Line. The best version for you will be tied to your True Story, with a clear outcome stated at a specific point in time. It should be something that inspires you, something that you get energy from. It's best if it's not fear-based. CEOs have plenty to worry about without adding arbitrarily generated worries about deadlines they might miss.

> Just as effective business leaders put strategy before tactics, traversing your journey as a CEO with a specific end in mind will serve you well. Knowing where you plan to go fuels intention in your daily life and gives you a perspective that will improve your decision-making.

A Finish Line re-enforces purpose. It can be a temporal "why" for you on the path to growing your business, something specific that drives urgency in your day, week, quarter, or year.

It might be a personal milestone related to wealth, retirement, or expansion of your influence or title. Shared Finish Lines—for example, taking the business public with an IPO—have the added benefit of inspiring and aligning your team. In that case, make sure and create it with your team's input. Finish Lines that are assigned are less powerful than those you build together.

What is your Next Race?

It's human nature to see the Finish Line as the end, but it rarely is. I've worked with many CEOs who get to their defined destination and find that there's a lot more life on the other side of the goal. Think of crossing your Finish Line as more of a graduation than an ending.

Which means you need to create a new Finish Line. Reflect on the race you just completed. Learn from it as you set the next target. Should it be broader or narrower? Could it be more aggressive, more aspirational, or more achievable? Will you include more or fewer people in the vision this time?

There's a spectrum here of frequency: how long are your races? You could have a grand goal for this business, with a far-off Finish Line—one that you see as the end for you and your company. On the other extreme, you could think of your MVP sprints as Finish Lines with weekly reinvention. The timeframe you choose for your Finish Lines will change their function and value for you and your team. Intentionally set it to help you achieve your goals.

Why Meaning Lasts

Most Accidental CEOs I know care about their legacy. They are not in this for transactional wins. They focus on their team and culture. They are working to put something in motion that will carry on long after they're gone.

In his book *Good to Great*, Jim Collins talks about Level Five Leaders who put their company's success above personal recognition. CMP Growth is like that. When you prioritize shared meaning, the purpose of your business, you are investing in something that can continue without you. The more you give of yourself to your business and its mission, the more you leave for it to continue the journey.

The best way to ensure your legacy is to let go of it. Rather than focusing on what you'll gain or keep when it's "over," focus on what you can instill in your business with your effort, your decisions, and your example every day. The good news is that when you share yourself, you don't lose yourself. Rather, both you and the company grow.

CHAPTER #9

Radical Clarity in Action

These Accidental CEOs' journeys are unique, but they each are riding the waves of CMP Growth in their own way to grow.

It's one thing to talk about Accidental CEOs using the power of clarity to surface meaning and activate purpose to transform themselves and their business; it's another to see real-world examples of this process in action. Here are three case studies of Accidental CEOs who have uncovered their truth, deployed their core meaning throughout their business, and leveraged that purpose as a unifying force to scale their businesses.

These leaders are currently in Wave 3 of their implementation of CMP Growth. While these case studies don't dwell on Wave 4, all three CEOs have started thinking about their Finish Lines and what happens next. This early work to sustain meaning as a legacy is already bearing fruit for them as they redefine their goals and revise their expectations about what comes after that.

Software Test Service Provider

This CEO's two-year-old business needed to scale fast. They had achieved $1M in annual revenue, with a goal to triple that in the next year. The company had proven it could solve the most challenging test processes for the world's largest software businesses but was struggling to take its business to the next level. They needed to expand the business beyond their network into some of the world's largest companies. They'd seen sales and marketing make a huge impact for others but didn't know how to build the kind of growth engine that could get them access to major enterprise clients for their business.

This first-time CEO also struggled with leadership challenges: sharing his vision, aligning the team, and building a high-performance, scalable organization.

Wave 1: Uncover Meaning

The story they were telling to the market was about their capabilities. They struggled to get prospects' attention, and theirs was a complicated story to tell. When they did connect, they found themselves competing with many "standard" providers.

We clarified the CEO's values and how they were directly linked to the company's mission. That alignment with the CEO's values injected new energy and direction for him and the growing team.

We used the Truth Chain process to craft a True Story that meaningfully connected the CEO, the team, and their value to prospects. This message elevated their message and got them noticed by their much larger target accounts. It also differentiated its offer from other providers. What had looked like just another testing service became one-of-a-kind and justified a premium price.

Wave 2: Deploy Meaning

It was clear that success would come from very few, very large enterprises. Because of this, they built their GPS Growth Engine around an Account-Based Marketing strategy and process to sharply target, reach, and engage the right people in the right organizations with their offer.

We uncovered a powerful, unique market position they were able to fully own. That two-word phrase instantly resonated with Fortune 100 software executives and spread their message readily within their enterprise target accounts. Its traction led to winning a multi-million dollar contract with a Fortune 50 firm within a few months—a testament to the ability of the right message to travel far, even when the message is from a tiny tech firm.

> Account-Based Marketing (ABM) is a Sales and Marketing strategy that focuses customer acquisition on a small number of strategic accounts. It is an effective approach for Tech B2B businesses that have a short list of high-value accounts in their target market.
>
> ABM "flips the funnel." Rather than bringing in as many leads as possible and filtering them down to become customers, ABM goes deep on a few

> accounts, expanding engagement and sales in each over time. Instead of working to be found by accounts, ABM identifies them first and then proactively pursues them.

Wave 3: Scale Meaning

At this point, growth was not an issue. It was building a coherent team and processes that could survive and thrive as the business rapidly scaled.

We implemented a Revenue Office to synchronize Operations, Sales, and Marketing that would support them in scaling the business to $100M in revenue. That Revenue Office proved critical because it gave these business "newbies" a structure to lean on as they repeatedly faced first-time challenges both internally and externally.

The CEO learned to rely less on his technical experience and more on his values and the company's True Story to guide growth and address issues and opportunities. Relying on his values and the company's True Story, instead of technical know-how, proved especially important in high-tension interpersonal situations with his team. With his radically clear True Story as an anchor, he has broken through personal and professional roadblocks to lead his talented and high-spirited employees as part of an aligned, collaborative team.

Property Technology Solutions Provider

This company was further along the path towards growth. In recent years, they had doubled revenue and were now approaching $10 million annually. Their biggest challenge was shifting their business to a more scalable model.

The business provided a property optimization platform for large real estate companies with contracts that typically ran more than $1M annually per client. The challenge was that their clients saw them as a site-by-site service provider rather than as a strategic business platform. That perception limited their ability to grow across their client's locations and operational functions.

Wave 1: Uncover Meaning

An important insight came to light when we looked at their target market. They had been opportunistic and dabbled in several real estate-related segments. We discovered that the single segment where they had the most success was more than large enough to support an incredibly large business scale. This sharp focus was difficult for the CEO to commit to, but once decided, this direction quickly led to even faster growth. They did less and did it better!

As their True Story took shape, it was clear that their focus on their transactional legacy deliveries clouded their messaging. By reframing the business around their platform that enables organization-wide value and relegating the transactional work as a lower-level add-on option that partners could also provide, they were able to articulate their unique and strategically valuable role. More focus and more clarity accelerated their business further.

Wave 2: Deploy Meaning

As we looked closer at their industry, we discovered a breakout opportunity: create and own a totally new category of enterprise solutions. Launching a new category would normally be prohibitively expensive and difficult. In their case, there were no competing solutions for this strategic corporate-wide application, and they had strong, sustainable differentiation. They decided to commit to this as their unique positioning.

The new category was well-received by clients and industry experts. So far, the new positioning has helped quicken their expansion in existing accounts and has opened the door to new accounts. They had a long journey ahead of them to develop and dominate this category, but they believed the opportunity was worth the risk and effort.

Wave 3: Scale Meaning

The CEO was skilled as a leader; the company had clear values, and the team was made up of highly qualified and motivated people. The Accidental CEO's hiring focus had been product development and delivery, and the scrappy and talented team was a key reason for their success.

Outside of the product team, many people were in part-time and/or temporary roles, and as the company grew, the leader struggled to scale this piecemeal approach. Cracks started appearing in performance and culture.

The CEO enlisted outside help to shift their People process and organization to be more structured and scalable. Jobs were better defined, and the CEO delegated some of the hiring. The company used the Entrepreneurial Operating System (EOS) to help them systematically implement these changes.

The company is on track to double revenue in the next year, and despite expected but unpredictable bumps in the road, its True Story and vision of category leadership will keep them aligned and motivated.

Medical Device Manufacturer

This company manufactured critical components for the medical systems industry. The first-time president had taken over the role as part of an employee-led buyout and was looking to accelerate growth—especially with their most important customers, the large medical systems providers that manufacture MRI, CT, and X-ray systems.

He was struggling with how to get beyond their dependence on contract manufacturing orders that didn't exploit the considerable value they could provide to design, build, and launch medical device subsystems. He could see their potential but felt stuck in their past.

Wave 1: Uncover Meaning

When I first visited this medical device company's website, they looked like a highly-capable parts manufacturer. That was an accurate description of the business, but it didn't tell the whole story—their True Story.

We uncovered their important and unique role: they were the industry's expert on patient interfaces. This identity anchored everything they did and highlighted their valuable contribution to helping these large systems providers elevate the patient experience—a key competitive advantage and a benefit to society.

Wave 2: Deploy Meaning

This new identity resonated with the president, and he used it effectively to strengthen the company culture and attract difficult-to-find workers as the business expanded. They also used the story to elevate their outreach to their strategic customers, helping the business overcome their reputation as just a parts maker and engaging with these key clients as a strategic partner in optimizing their complex systems.

The company also implemented an Account-Based Marketing strategy to target these higher-level opportunities systematically. By creating value-added content related to their expertise in patient interfaces, they were able to get past Procurement and engage with designers, product managers, and others who valued their contributions.

We uncovered their important and unique role: they were the industry's expert on patient interfaces. This identity anchored everything they did and highlighted their valuable contribution to helping these large systems providers elevate the patient experience—a key competitive advantage and a benefit to society.

Wave 3: Scale Meaning

The president further clarified the business as it grew by embracing the 80/20 Rule as a strategic business tool. They evaluated the profitability and volume of every product, radically reducing the number of parts that they offered to clients. This focus freed up time and resources for the company to focus on growth areas without any negative impact on profitability.

The business recently expanded capacity with a large factory in Mexico, giving more flexibility in supporting its steady-state contract manufacturing work while it invests in expanding its full-spectrum patient interface solutions. The president hired a COO, which has helped him focus more on leading the team and the business.

Common Threads in Clarity

These Accidental CEOs' journeys are unique, but they each are riding the waves of CMP Growth in their own way to grow. Each leader has grown individually, both personally and professionally. Their businesses have expanded aggressively and are scaling effectively. Importantly, all three of these companies see continued growth ahead. Their markets are targeted, but still provide a lot of room for them to become much more.

The concept of ABM was transformative for all three businesses. ABM is not right for every B2B firm; your company may not have the concentrated account landscape that makes it so valuable. But if you do see less than 100 accounts making or breaking your future, consider adopting this strategy.

All three of these companies firmly believe in what they do. Their Finish Line is not just a dollar sign. These leaders see things differently than they did when they first took on the CEO role, and that new perspective has given them more confidence in their future as they move forward in their dynamic and uncertain markets.

I've witnessed many business leaders transformed by the concepts behind the CMP Growth Waves. I wish the same for you.

CHAPTER #10

How Accidental CEOs Get in Their Own Way

You don't have to do things the way you have in the past; you don't have to do things like everyone else.

I hope you are feeling hopeful at this point. I hope you see that the limitations tied to your inexperience as a businessperson don't prevent you from achieving unbounded success and, someday, finishing this exciting and meaningful adventure well.

I've found that early in the CMP Growth process, CEOs are generally excited. They see more clearly the meaning of their venture. Their team gets it, too, and this newfound clarity and purpose brings alignment and energy to everyone. Things look brighter; people are more determined to succeed.

If you're starting to feel some of this, savor it. There will be ups and downs in this journey as you ride the Waves together. It takes commitment to stay the course through the highs and lows to reap the rewards of the CMP Growth Waves. Sadly, I've seen Accidental CEOs start strong but lose their way.

They Don't Take It Seriously

One path to failure with the CMP Growth Waves starts at the very beginning: the CEO doesn't really believe in the power of meaning. They view this process as just another marketing exercise and are skeptical that their customers really care about anything other than cost and capabilities.

Meaning Doesn't Take Root

For these leaders, uncovering their truth in Wave 1 produces uneven results because they often aren't getting to the real situation. They resist the vulnerability of digging for what's really happening and not happening in their business and the market. It's hard work that can challenge their beliefs; it's not for the faint of heart. They instead settle for messages that will persuade or even manipulate their customers to act in their favor.

> This kind of True Story is brittle and weak. At the first sign of trouble—poor revenue results, product quality issues, new competition—the Story is changed or replaced with a totally different approach.

They succumb to these shortcuts and build a story that isn't based on the truth but on how they think it will influence their prospects. They are staying at the surface.

Shallow Roots Can't Withstand Stress

This kind of True Story is brittle and weak. At the first sign of trouble—poor revenue results, product quality issues, new competition—the Story is changed or replaced with a totally different approach. It might not even be trouble that changes things; the stress of success—the changing dynamics of your growing team or a major account win—can cause your True Story to be cast aside for something shiny and new.

It's sometimes hard to see this happening. You may continue working through the CMP Growth process, giving lip service to each step. The business spends a lot of time and effort developing strategies and initiatives that are based on that lip service.

These plans are built and deployed in an empty shell. Your results from all of that investment are modest or worse. Your team becomes disengaged because they see that the business's words don't match actions; they are working and living a lie.

When your True Story is based not on truth but on manufactured ideas, it can't survive.

They Don't Trust the Process

Another road to ruin for Accidental CEOs on the journey to purposeful growth is subtle: they see the value of their strong new message, but they don't trust it. After a robust start, they drift away from their unique path and lose the power of their story.

Playing It Safe

These CEOs start strong. They find their clear truth and see its value for the business. As long as there is no resistance, they make great progress: they bring their team on board and even start deploying shared meaning in their business. But at some point, there will be a challenge, and these Accidental CEOs will then question their direction.

Usually, it's a slow and steady shift away from their True Story. They seek extensive feedback from their team members or outside experts; they confuse the process of gaining alignment with a popularity contest and make modifications to soften the edges and remove challenging points to the story.

Commoditized Meaning

The effect of these compromises-by-committee is that the message loses its strength. The pure story uncovered in Wave 1 gets watered down and no longer engages their bullseye customers. They don't appear to be one-of-a-kind and may even start to look and sound just like everyone else.

> Accidental CEOs who lose faith in their truth and compromise to play things safe lose their market power. They are back to fighting in the trenches for attention and commitment from prospects.

Just as commoditized markets drive product prices down, commoditized meaning drives attraction down. With a few minor edits, their True Story becomes just another story that gets lost in the noise.

Businesses Can't Defy Gravity

The only way for businesses to stand out is to take a risk. If you find your truth, that becomes a well-calculated risk—one that you need to be willing to take because that's who you are. If your business tries to be something it's not, it will still fail, just in a different way. Accidental CEOs who lose faith in their truth and compromise to play things safe lose their market power. They are back to fighting in the trenches for attention and commitment from prospects.

These businesses may have a better message than before and will likely get a bump in performance based on the Wave 1 work. But the benefit is short-lived. As they slide back into Conventionalville, their growth stalls again. The team becomes more cynical and eventually disengages as the new ideas devolve into the same old ones.

They Can't Handle Growth

The final scenario to watch out for comes from the unexpected consequences of success. For some Accidental CEOs, growing the business with radical clarity is not the problem; it's adapting to the changes that come with growth.

Early Success

These leaders have a transformative experience in the early Waves of CMP Growth. They find their powerful True Story, and it works; employees rally around it, and the team gels. Priorities and conversations shift into alignment around their customers and are less about the business.

Their shared meaning guides them to a clear and very specific target segment. Their message spreads easily to their bullseye customers. Prospects increasingly seek them out. Growth accelerates.

The Challenges of Scale

But change, even positive change, is stressful. New challenges appear, and while they are "champagne problems" born of success, they are still thorny and difficult to solve.

As the team grows, interpersonal dynamics shift. New conflicts surface between teammates; departments start to deal with tribal tendencies. The business may struggle to hire the right people and stress the culture of the business.

> They had expected that once the business solved the growth dilemma, things would get easier. The stress and overwhelm continues unabated. And while Accidental CEOs are not afraid of hard work, they can lose confidence that they can maintain control as things grow even bigger.

The impact of the CEO's decisions has grown, too. There is more at stake with every investment. Hunches are more risky; the CEO has to be more deliberate and yet more efficient because there are more decisions to make. And how does the leader share the decision-making without the business spinning out of control?

They Don't Evolve

Some CEOs go astray at this point. They had expected that once the business solved the growth dilemma, things would get easier. The stress and overwhelm continues unabated. And while Accidental CEOs are not afraid of hard work, they can lose confidence that they can maintain control as things grow even bigger.

These CEOs that fall off of the CMP Growth Waves 3 or 4 lose control because they try to hold on too tightly. They lose focus on their True Story, which means that everyone else does, too. They deal tactically with personnel and operational issues without viewing them through the lens of their mission. Their marketing and sales efforts start to look more like everyone else's.

These are three paths that CEOs can go down and lose their way; there are others. The good news is that if you choose to take this journey, you have practical tools to help you navigate a variety of scenarios on this wild but wonderful ride. These tools will help you continue to act in concert with your mission, no matter what occurs.

You don't have to do things the way you have in the past; you don't have to do things like everyone else. In fact, your priceless asset is your True Story, which gives you a script for success, unlike absolutely everyone else. It's what this journey is all about.

YOUR NEXT STEPS

As an Accidental CEO, you are extraordinary. I don't mean this as a vague, unfounded compliment; I don't know you, really. But if you meet the profile of a technical expert who is taking on the mantle of a business leader because of your vision for what it can be, you are choosing a path that sets you apart.

You have an exceptional opportunity. Think of everything that brought you to this role and all of the possibilities that stand before you. Few leaders ever reach this point; it is truly rare air—congratulations!

Now, what will you do with it?

If you don't act to break down the conflicts and confusion within yourself and in your business that cloud the horizon for Accidental CEOs, things will continue as is. Stubborn issues will resurface over and over. Unexpected challenges will disorient you and disrupt your team. You will struggle to get your business to stand out in your market and be seen for what you really are: the one and only alternative for this thing that you do so well. You might succeed based on financial metrics, but will you capture the full potential of this moment?

Make Room for Meaning

I hope you now see that there is a path to achieving your goals and fully realizing what your business can become. Change starts the moment you change the script.

It's not doing more, only louder; it's doing less better, quietly discovering what exactly it is that you and your business can bring to the world and for precisely whom. It's uncovering that truth and implanting it in the hearts and minds of others on the journey with you. That clarity of purpose, once it's found and activated in your business, will drive the engine of growth.

The sharper that clarity is, the faster your message can spread into the market and the more it strikes a chord with your best prospects. Your story's authenticity and value accelerate their journey to actualize it. Trust is more readily formed, and commitments are more easily made. Revenue, profit, and passion grow.

Your clarity of purpose is also the glue that holds things together as you chaotically scale. Growth is hard work; the importance of every decision grows, too. With your clear mission embedded throughout your organization and reinforced by you as you personally live it, your company can overcome the stresses and even thrive on the exciting path to success.

The clarity of your mission also has the staying power to remain when you are gone. Your departure may be in three years or fifty. Your clarity-turned-meaning-turned-purpose will evolve within the venture in whatever form it takes after you've left the ring, but the golden nugget of value and truth that you helped create will live on. Your legacy endures.

Elbow Grease: Do the Work

All it takes is to start small and start now. Set aside time to slow down and give clarity the space it needs to do its work. Use the tools in this book to start your journey. Take a step at a time. Move on only when you're confident that you've got a grasp on that topic, but don't wait for things to be perfect to move on to the next thing. MVP everything.

Don't tackle this alone. You can't force meaning into the hearts of your teammates. By uncovering it together with your trusted partners first and expanding the circle over time, you will not only gain their unified support, but you'll have invaluable help in moving this forward. It will be less lonely and far more productive.

The process is not rocket science, but it does take effort and commitment. If you do the work and stick with it, you can unite your team, grow your business, and leave a lasting legacy.

It's Your Choice

There is nothing more powerful than pure, unadulterated meaning. You'll never achieve perfection, but the closer you get to the truth, the more value you unlock. Think of the value Starbucks generated from a new idea of what a coffee shop could be. Or how Google changed the world with a new way to look for things. Or the immense wealth generated by Amazon for changing the definition of "bookstore."

The meaning behind your company has unbounded potential. You may not achieve it; the market might not be there now, or there's something else in the way that you won't see without moving forward. But isn't it worth the effort to evolve as a CEO to try?

Given your background, your outlook, and your influential leadership role, you have a rare opportunity to discover if your dream can change the world. Regardless of the outcome of your venture, you will gain much from the journey if you choose to take it. You are in the right place at the right time with valuable insights, an informed outlook, and the commitment to try.

I wish you confidence and success on your journey to clarity, meaning, and growth!

What To Do Next

If you see the potential for CMP Growth to help you accelerate your journey, your best move is to take a small step now towards your bigger future. Don't let the spark die out; even a simple act will bring progress and keep you moving forward. Here are three suggestions:

Take the Accidental CEO Audit

We talked about this tool in Chapter 5. It's an easy step to personal clarity around where you stand today on Leadership, Strategy, Growth, Alignment, and Culture.

Scan the QR code here:

b2b-clarity.com/accidental-ceo-audit

Radical Clarity Bonus Resources

Another strong step forward is to work through the CMP Growth Wave frameworks from the book that resonated with you while they are still fresh in your mind. Abstract concepts deliver more value when they are made personally relevant. Download these worksheets, which will guide you through frameworks from the book and pull these ideas into your world so they can work for you.

Scan the QR code here:

b2b-clarity.com/resources

Schedule a Clarity Call

If you're an Accidental CEO ready to take concrete steps to accelerate your growing business, schedule a Clarity Call with me. In this 30-minute session, we'll discuss your situation, and I'll provide specific ideas on how to move your unique business forward.

Scan the QR code here:

b2b-clarity.com/contact

Whatever you decide to do, the secret to success is to do it. Clarity and growth come from intentional action pointed in the general direction of your Truth.

ABOUT THE AUTHOR

Pete Steege helps business leaders break through uncertainty and build momentum. As the creator of the CMP Growth framework and founder of B2B Clarity, he guides technical experts on their journey from Accidental CEOs to confident, purpose-driven leaders. With decades of experience across industries and company sizes, Pete equips leaders with the clarity, strategy, and tools to scale their businesses and leave a lasting impact.

BOOKS BY PETE STEEGE

On Purpose: The CEO's Guide to Marketing With Meaning

Marketing isn't something you do, it's part of who you are.

Many B2B CEOs carry a dark secret: their marketing is broken—and they don't know how to fix it. Pete Steege's groundbreaking book, *On Purpose*, offers an unexpected solution: focus first on why you are marketing, and the results will follow. He reframes B2B marketing around a purposeful mindset that helps business leaders rightsize their campaigns, align their teams, and have more impact with less angst and effort.

Using this accessible and usable guide, you will learn:

- What marketing can and can't do for your business.
- How much you should spend on marketing—and where.
- Which marketing tactics are right for your company.
- Why your most powerful message isn't about you.

Steege shares his experience from three decades as a global marketing leader for innovative companies, ranging from Silicon Valley startups to large corporations. *On Purpose* will change how you think about marketing—and help you and your business achieve your boldest goals.

Radical Clarity: How Accidental CEOs Unlock Meaning, Lead with Purpose, and Accelerate Growth

Many technical experts become CEOs by accident—thrown into leadership without a roadmap. But true success isn't just about running a business—it's about leading with purpose, scaling with confidence, and leaving a lasting legacy.

In *Radical Clarity*, Pete Steege unveils the Clarity-Meaning-Purpose (CMP) Growth framework: the proven path from expert to visionary leader. You'll discover how to:

- Craft a compelling leadership story that attracts the right opportunities.
- Build a clear, strategic roadmap that ignites growth and momentum.

- Scale your business with confidence—without losing control or burning out.
- Cement your influence and create a legacy that outlasts you.

Packed with real-world insights and hard-won lessons, ***Radical Clarity*** is your guide to stepping up, standing out, and building something that truly matters.